Margit Kovács

Margit Kovács

ILONA
PATAKY-BRESTYÁNSZKY

Margit Kovács

CORVINA KIADÓ
KÉPZŐMŰVÉSZETI ALAP KIADÓVÁLLALATA
BUDAPEST

Title of the Hungarian original:
Kovács Margit
Képzőművészeti Alap Kiadóvállalata — Corvina Kiadó, Budapest, 1976
First Hungarian edition © P. Brestyánszky Ilona, 1976

Translated by Susanna Horn
Translation revised by Elisabeth West
The illustration material was compiled by
Ilona Pataky-Brestyánszky
Colour photographs: Alfréd Schiller
Black-and-white photographs: Károly Gink, Ferenc Haár,
Judit Kárász, István Petrás and the archives of Margit Kovács
Design by Mariann Gelányi

© Ilona Pataky-Brestyánszky, 1976
ISBN 963 13 0677 1 — ISBN 963 336 197 4

On the front cover: *Nursing Mother*
On the back cover: *"Fluctuat nec mergitur". Jug*

Second edition

The Art of Margit Kovács

Humanism, a delight in beauty and craftsmanship, a reverence for the nature of her chosen medium and virtuosity of technique—these are the traits which characterize the works of Margit Kovács. István Gádor, Géza Gorka and Margit Kovács can be said to have created the art of modern Hungarian pottery. This frail woman—the youngest of the group—was relentless in her determination, worked with equal success in the round and in reliefs, in designing pictures to be engraved on clay tiles and in using the potter's wheel to make ornamental ceramics, and she had a rare gift for mixing glazes of delicate shades.

In all her work Margit Kovács's vision was centred on the life of man. Her themes are many and varied, for her work includes portraits in a realistic tone, serious biblical compositions, brilliantly characterized grotesque figures and conversation pieces, scenes of men at work, vivid illustrations of folk songs, and richly decorated pitchers and dishes. Her art has a uniquely individual tone, yet it is rooted in Hungarian traditions, and it is also universal in its humanism. Her idiom of forms and her artistic creed can be traced to *art nouveau (Sezession)*, the style which dominated the years around 1900, terminating one epoch and ushering in the next.

Margit Kovács was born in 1902, at Győr, a small Transdanubian town richly endowed with historical associations. The years of her childhood corresponded with the end of the Francis Joseph period of the Austro-Hungarian Monarchy. Already during the last decades of the nineteenth century Hungary was developing as a nation and progress was especially evident in the rapidly growing capital city of Budapest. The bourgeoisie, having acquired power, quickly made up for the lost time in developing a capitalist social system; they created a liberal and cosmopolitan atmosphere in which economic and intellectual developments took place simultaneously.

In Hungary the closing years of the century were characterized by confusion. It was a time of profound contradictions and the new country was the scene of many trends. It was possible to discern the first warning signs of a scientific-technical revolution, while the rapid development of industry was followed by radical changes in the class structure of society. The old, existing framework of life was disrupted by the growth of large towns with their much faster rhythm of life. Liberalism proclaimed the unbounded freedom of the individual: "The individual demands liberty to create the new art which satisfies the age and the people among whom it takes shape..."[1] The new trend of art, which was spreading through Europe, now reached Hungary too.

The whole of cultural life was imbued with the ideas of the *art nouveau;* every aspect of every branch of art was affected as well as attitudes to art. The fight between progress and bigotry dominated contemporary taste and the development of the arts. It was only World War I which brought to a halt this tremendous effort to evolve a universal, all-embracing new style representing the age.

In an epoch when style was of such concern to everyone associated with the applied arts, what did this mean for Central Europe, and for Hungary in particular? Some explanation has been given by the art historian Lajos Németh who says, "... besides the search for grand art, the grand style, the aim was to bring forth against the radiant background of the Millennium a mainly ornamental style of strongly national character which, while conceived in a cosmopolitan spirit, left room for the decoration and construction of the Székely gates of Transylvania, for erotic romanticism, a longing for death and a love of mysticism; *art nouveau* was to be applied to goods produced commercially, there was to be a place for a nostalgic style using the mystical colouring of the great masters of opposing styles, an opportunity to formulate an aesthetics of industry that would capture unerringly the style of socialist reality; there was to be a reflection of the writings of Ruskin and Oscar Wilde on art, a place for Nietzsche as well as the underground railway, the buildings of Ödön Lechner, the Museum of Applied Arts, the edifice of the Post Office Savings Bank, Zsolnay majolica, and Álmos Jaschik."[2] What, if anything, could Margit Kovács perceive of all this in the sleepy Transdanubian provincial town where she grew up? What she in fact saw were the everyday pleasures and cares of ordinary people, especially their industry and their hard struggle to survive in difficult conditions. Her father, a teacher, died when she was still a child, her mother became head-mistress of a boys' boarding-school and the young girl soon learnt how difficult it was to make both ends meet.

Margit Kovács's artistic talent soon became apparent. She responded sensitively to her surroundings. She stored in her memory images of villagers as they moved to and fro, peasant women carrying heavy bundles, the brightly coloured forms of carts transporting animals, the lively bustle of the market, the bright vegetable stalls, the apple-women and the fishwives; cherished throughout her childhood, these memories would all be recalled later as symbols of the perpetual motion of life and depicted one day in her works. Drawing was her medium, and it was in lines that she tried to express her experiences. In the street where she lived as a child there was a stove builder who noticed the little girl's sense of form; he it was who made her familiar with clay, which was to become the basic material of her art.

After leaving her secondary school, she tried to get a post in a bank to earn her living. However, her family, realizing that she showed promise as an artist, decided to spare neither effort nor expense to make it possible for her to study art in Budapest.

She found her way to Álmos Jaschik, one of the finest draughtsmen of early twentieth century. Soon after 1920, Jaschik had opened a private school for training artists, many of whom became pioneers in the development of modern Hungarian graphic art and the applied arts. Jaschik's style left an indelible mark on the applied graphic art of the early decades of the century. His principal interest was the illustration of books; his illuminations of the poems of Sándor Petőfi and Endre Ady are works of enduring value, in which decadence, symbolism and decoratively stylized reality are all unmistakable elements. In his work we find the capricious lines of the *art nouveau*, a stylized toying with decorative lines, in which the elements of folk art are also discernible, and a tension deriving from a rich and varied rhythm of movement, qualities which have made his works the most typical products of European *art nouveau*. The nervous, delicate movements of the figures in his illustrations were inspired by the drawings of Walter Crane, William Morris and Aubrey Vincent Beardsley, while reflecting also the influence of the Vienna *art nouveau* group centred round the magazine *Ver Sacrum*, of whom Emil Orlik was the most dominant figure.

In Vienna and Budapest the *art nouveau* movement set in almost simultaneously and was adopted with all the vigour of youth: it implied revolt against academicism, modernity and social progress.

Álmos Jaschik advocated the synthesis of various branches of art, an idea highly characteristic of the *art nouveau*. His pupils, including Margit Kovács, were imbued with this spirit. The theory which became the ideological foundation of the *art nouveau* had been formulated in the middle of the nineteenth century by the English Pre-Raphaelites, John Ruskin, Dante Gabriel Rossetti, William Holman Hunt, John Everett Millais, Edward Burne-Jones and William Morris. The economic basis of Pre-Raphaelitism was the great leap in economic-industrial progress, with Great Britain leading the way. With the spread of manufacturing industry aesthetic standards for utilitarian objects declined sharply, for the chief aim of manufacturers was to satisfy quantitative demands. In the production of objects for everyday use, all consideration of appearance, choice of material, suitability of shape, and the traditions of the early guilds of craftsmen, were disregarded. New methods of production, newly introduced materials, revolutionary technological processes, all demanded new planning and aesthetic solutions. This was one of the most important characteristics of the development of the *art nouveau* movement, and later, of twentieth century applied arts.

It was the social reformer Morris, with his pioneering ideas about aesthetics, who applied Ruskin's aesthetic creed, "beauty is our daily bread", which finally degenerated into an expression of the decadent mentality of the too subtle bourgeois élite of the close of the century. William Morris transplanted his tenets into reality in his textile workshop and printing press, the Kelmscott Press. Morris and Ruskin were surrounded by a whole group of eminent artist-craftsmen (Ch. R. Ashbee, Ch. Mackintosh, etc.). In cooperation with the group, the English Arts and Crafts Movement promoted the development of *art nouveau* motifs—the abstract dynamism of lines, the mingling of organic vegetable forms with static-geometrical elements. The sources of this renewal of forms were heterogeneous: Italian fifteenth century painting, Japanese art and, in the countries of East Central Europe, to a considerable extent, folk art as well.

The works of Álmos Jaschik also derived from the outlook prevailing among the Hungarian upper middle classes at the turn of the century. The master implanted among his pupils the creed of "beauty is our daily bread", a creed to which Margit Kovács has remained faithful throughout her life. Jaschik also formulated a unique theory of art, the basis of which was the spiral line symbolizing life. (The gently undulating spiral line is the most typical external characteristic of the *art nouveau*.)

Margit Kovács's first intention was to devote herself to graphic art; accordingly, she was given assignments for posters, packaging, the illustration or illumination and binding of books and for book jackets. She attended Jaschik's school during the years 1922–26. It was not only drawing that she practised; together with a friend, Judit Kende, who later became a ceramist, she tried her hand at painting porcelain—very fashionable at that time among the bourgeoisie of Budapest—in the workshop of the Budapest College of Applied Arts. But she was not attracted to this form of art and her experience only confirmed her in her attachment to ceramics.

In 1926, like so many artists and writers of her generation, she went to Vienna for further training. Their state of mind is epitomized in the words of the writer and poet István Vas who, when setting out for Vienna in 1929, wrote that, "... from our semi-feudal semi-capitalist 'Fallowland' she was travelling to the 'cultural West'"[3].

In spite of the disintegration of the Habsburg Empire, Hungarian cultural life was still closely linked to that of the former capital of the Austro-Hungarian Monarchy, Vienna, which, after the collapse of the Republic of Councils in 1919, gave asylum to Hungarian progressive intellectuals. There was a stratum of the urban middle classes for whom Vienna was the cultural and social Mecca. In the sphere of applied arts, Vienna was, indeed, a focal point of progress in Europe, for it was the home of the Wiener Werkstätte, which was so important for every branch of contemporary applied art in East Central Europe, particularly for the art of ceramics. The foundation of the Wiener Werkstätte is inseparable from the name of Josef Hoffmann, a notable personality of the *art nouveau* in Vienna who, together with Gustav Klimt (leader of the *sezessionist* artists there), Kolo Moser and Fritz Wärndorfer, businessman and patron of art, respectively, founded this centre for the applied arts in the year 1903. The Wiener Werkstätte carried further the idea of the "workshop" advanced by the Pre-Raphaelites. The artists who worked there strove to create new forms for utensils in daily use, furniture, cutlery and objects for interior decoration; their aim was to create a new harmony between architecture and interior decoration, a new unity in the environment of man. Individual pieces were produced, but series were also planned. During the first decade of the century over a hundred workmen and thirty master-craftsmen were active in the workshops.

During the period when Margit Kovács was studying there, the architect Dagobert Peche was the life and soul of the Wiener Werkstätte. His work, which greatly influenced artists active during the second phase of the Wiener Werkstätte in the decade following World War I, was equally significant for the applied arts of contemporary Vienna. His playful, imaginative, amply decorative forms and effortless elegance exerted a powerful influence on the artist-craftsmen of the workshops. Dagobert Peche played an important role in the eclectic trend of the twenties, Art Deco, in which there was a merging of several styles. This tendency, while retaining more constructive and comprehensive elaboration of forms and a certain classicism, drew on the *art nouveau* for intensively stylized decorative endeavours (as indicated by the name of the movement); however, in colouring there were other, more powerful influences. Another characteristic feature of Art Deco was the use of folk art elements which, corresponding to the realities of society in Hungary after World War I, were increasingly associated with Hungarian applied arts. The impact of Art Deco is discernible in the creative activity of the most eminent artist-craftsmen in Hungary in the years between the two world wars, demonstrated in the sphere of ceramics by István Gádor, Géza Gorka and Margit Kovács.

There was also close cooperation between artists of the Wiener Werkstätte and Michael Powolny, Professor of the Vienna College of Applied Arts, under whom Margit Kovács intended to study in Vienna. It was in the spirit of the *art nouveau* that Powolny advocated the renewal and elevation to a nobler plane of the traditional handicraft of glazed pottery. His own work was greatly influenced by African plastic art. It was due to Powolny that the store of forms and motifs associated with the Wiener Werkstätte was enriched by the art of the African peoples as well as the ornamental world peculiar to the *art nouveau*.

István Gádor, creator of modern Hungarian pottery, and a member of the Wiener Werkstätte in 1915, was responsible for introducing the ideas of the movement into Hungary. It was in 1921 that he first exhibited in Hungary his glazed pottery executed in the modern spirit. In 1926—the year when Margit Kovács set out for Vienna—Gádor's work was awarded a gold medal at the World Exhibition in Barcelona.[4]

In the countries of East Central Europe the modern art of ceramics was first introduced by pupils of the Wiener Werkstätte while Helena Johnova, who in 1919 became Professor of the School of Applied Arts in Prague, pioneered the art of modern ceramics in Czechoslovakia. The development of the art in Yugoslavia benefited from the traditional Bohemian craft of glazed pottery; and a link with the Wiener Werkstätte was forged through the works of Hinko Juhn who became the founding figure of modern Yugoslav ceramic art after finishing his training at the School of Glazed Pottery in Teplice.

The scientific experiments of French ceramists have played an important part in the emergence of modern glazed pottery. Starting with the idea of reviving historical styles, ever since the middle of the 19th century French experts have been studying these styles and they have rediscovered techniques of pottery which had long been forgotten. Charles-Antoine Avisseau unravelled the secret of Palissy faience with its decoration of naturalistic animals and plants applied in relief; this dates from the period of the French Renaissance and profoundly influenced the art of glazed pottery in Central Europe during the second half of the nineteenth century. Pieces of Palissy faience were manufactured by several factories in Europe including, in 1874, that owned by the Hungarian Vilmos Zsolnay[5]. Jules Claude Ziegler experimented with salt-glazed earthenware, while Joseph Theodore Deck of Alsace, the supreme master ceramist of his age, rediscovered for modern pottery a remarkable number of ceramic techniques of the Middle and Far East. A man passionately committed to research, he invented many new techniques and modes of ornamentation. At the World Exhibitions in the second half of the 19th century Deck was much acclaimed; his works were imitated all over Europe because their lavish decoration appealed to the taste for the oppressive type of luxury cultivated in interior decoration from the 1880s on.[6]

In this era of *art nouveau* pottery, when old styles were revived, the most prominent and individually active ceramists were the members of the French group L'Art du Feu[7]; exceptionally creative and active, they were also very influential. They battled for the recognition of individually created glazed pottery as an art, preparing the way for the artist-potters of the twentieth century.

The members of L'Art du Feu grouped themselves round E. Chaplet. They prepared stoneware (from very silicious clay: *grès*) burnt at high temperatures (and still the basic material of glazed pottery) which they decorated with high temperature glaze or varnish, as seen on monochrome and fluid *(flambé)* fire-baked glazed Chinese and Japanese stoneware.

It was in 1889 that Chaplet[8] first successfully created an ornamentation in the French style but based on Japanese prototypes. He was extremely skilful in his use of copper, blue, purple and white in every shade and variety. His forms were turned on the wheel, but he also reintroduced free-hand moulding; it was due to him that free-hand moulding became in Europe one of the most characteristic techniques of twentieth century artistic pottery. Every modern ceramist uses this technique, as does Margit Kovács, who combines it with the use of the potter's wheel.

In the school which gathered around Chaplet the most outstanding member was Auguste Delacherche[9], who took over Chaplet's workshop. He produced not only valuable utilitarian objects, but also designed types which could be turned out in series on a commercial basis.

The development of modern European pottery, in regard to technique as well as form, was determined by French ceramists. They were the first in the history of modern ceramics to make a conscious effort to eliminate the dividing line between the fine and the applied arts.

Adrien Dalpeyrat[10] and Edmond Lachenal[11] were also pupils of Chaplet. Dalpeyrat's works are characterized by the use of transparent glazes in dark-blue, crimson and yellow. Some of his vases are adorned with figures in relief. The Japanese influence can also be seen in the art of Edmond Lachenal.

Emile Lenoble was another artist associated with Chaplet[12]. He used *engobe* decorations and was a lively stylist, creating elaborate floral-lineal ornamentations. His vivid colours melted harmoniously into the grey hue of the *grès*.

Emile Decœur[13] bridged the transition to contemporary ceramics. His vessels are sparsely decorated, with only a couple of small reliefs shaped like written characters or the addition of one or two leaves. Glazes, generously applied, are held in fine tones. Surfaces are soft, creating a velvety impression. All Decœur's vases are free-hand mouldings.

It was in the workshops of Delacherche, Chaplet, Carries, Dalpeyrat, Lachenal, Lenoble and their associates that modern glazed pottery came into being, an art which offers a powerful medium for artistic expression while at the same time demanding craftsman-like techniques, and ranking equally with the fine arts. Their work was imitated all over Europe. They began by giving encouragement to factories and the small potters' workshops. For instance at Pécs in Vilmos Zsolnay's Works, the most widely known glazed-tile factory of the Austro-Hungarian Monarchy, a separate unit was set up to produce artistic glazed pottery in small series after the designs of Henrik Darilek, Géza Nikelszky and Lajos Mack.

Artists associated with the L'Art du Feu should be credited with the fact that a considerable number of famous artists were sufficiently interested in their work to begin to experiment with pottery. Members of the Nabis, who early recognized the significance of the applied arts, were the first to understand the perspectives inherent in glazed pottery[14]. Maurice Denis, Bonnard and Vuillard all made designs for applied arts. In Banyuls-sur-Mer, Maillol, the great sculptor, designed carpets; the Hungarian member of the group, József Rippl-Rónai, made designs for tapestry, furniture and glass objects as well as for glazed pottery.

Around 1900, a group of artists, close followers of Matisse, who were known collectively as Les Fauves, showed a marked interest in pottery, influenced mainly by the gifted French ceramist, André Metthey (1871–1921)[15], who died while still a young man. Metthey's friends—including Matisse, Rouault, Bonnard, Derain, Van Dongen, Vlaminck —painted plates, vases, sometimes even tea-sets. After World War I, Llorens Artigas[16], the Catalonian ceramist, who had moved to Paris, persuaded Braque, Dufy and Miró to take up glazed pottery.

Nevertheless ceramics failed to rouse widespread continuous interest among artists until it was taken up by Picasso, that supreme exponent of modern fine art. But from the year 1946 when Picasso[17] moulded his first small bull in the workshop of Georges Ramié at Vallauris, a former centre for pottery at that time in decline, there was a considerable renewal of interest. Today many contemporary artists, inspired by Picasso, seek a new means of artistic expression in ceramics.

In Paris exhibitions of glazed pottery by painters and sculptors followed one another in quick succession; artists strove to break through the barriers of ceramics, uniting sculpture with pictorial elements; and traditional pottery forms established for thousands of years were transformed for use in interior decoration.

In addition to those already mentioned, other famous artists who have produced glazed pottery in the twentieth century and who have thereby been a source of inspiration to ceramists, include Fernand Léger, Jean Lurçat, Georges Braque, Jean Cocteau, Van Dongen and the Hungarian Victor Vasarely.

The course pursued by Margit Kovács in her art was decided by Powolny who, being unable to admit her to his own class for lack of a place, introduced her to Hertha Bucher, a former colleague of István Gádor, a talented ceramist of the second generation of the Wiener Werkstätte. Eminent members of this generation, Wally Wieselthier, Gudrun Baudisch-Teltscher, Grete Kleinwalder, Viktor Lurje, Lucie Rie-Gomperz, Willy Russ, Susi Singer-Schimmerl and Julie Sitte, worked together with the Gmundener Keramische Werkstätte after the dissolution of the Wiener Werkstätte in the year 1932, the period when Margit Kovács was studying in Vienna[18]. Hertha Bucher had a small pottery workshop in an old one-storey house in the Mozart Gasse in Vienna. In an interview given to *Új Magyarság* in 1936 Margit Kovács spoke of her teacher in this tiny workshop "... there were no more than four or five pupils, which meant that they were very thoroughly trained by their teacher—who really knew how to kindle a love for ceramics."[19] Hertha Bucher revealed the new world of clay to Margit Kovács who enthusiastically delved into the secrets of the craft. From dawn to dusk, she kneaded figures and shaped vessels in the manner of her teacher.

After Álmos Jaschik it was the reserved Hertha Bucher, a woman who revealed her thoughts and feelings only in her work, who most influenced Margit Kovács both as a human being and as a craftsman: she it was who taught her a multiplicity of forms and all the latest techniques. Hertha Bucher was not only a good ceramist, but also a wonderful teacher. She moulded her figures on a potter's wheel, and this ancient instrument taught her pupils unlimited respect for their material. Her fresh, expressive modelling and technical efficiency was a major influence on Margit Kovács for more than ten years. She also made large pieces, for instance fireplaces; this, too, had an effect on the art of Margit Kovács.

Margit Kovács spent two years in Vienna. She became familiar with various trends of style and techniques of glazing which reached Vienna as the ideas and aspirations of L'Art du Feu became more widely known, particularly the use of fluid varnishes which were much favoured at the time and in the application of which Hertha Bucher excelled. When her hands were tired, Margit Kovács devoted what little time remained to studying the treasures in the museums. She was attracted by the art of ancient Greece and Rome; in the city of Vienna it was the Gothic splendour and mystical atmosphere of St. Stephen's cathedral that she most enjoyed and appreciated.

What was it that drew Margit Kovács to masterpieces so remote from our age? When asked in 1950, she replied, "I felt in them something very ancient and truthful, the charm of primitive expression, the delightfully balanced beauty of the compositions."[20]

The next stage in her training was Munich, where in 1928–29 she studied sculpture at the Staatsschule für Angewandte Kunst under Karl Killer and ceramics under Adalbert Niemeyer. Karl Killer produced religious works, his modelling always adapted to the nature of his material. It was here that Margit Kovács learnt to indicate her compositions by outlining her ideas as they came to her in tiny clumps of clay.

After returning home from Munich in 1929, she moved from Győr to Budapest where she began to associate with other Hungarian artists. During her years of study she had been so quick to learn the secrets of her craft that the works she had made in Vienna were exhibited, together with those of the painter János György Simon, at the Tamás Gallery in Budapest[21]. Critics found her work "remarkably artistic". Also in 1928 she took part in the June Group Show of the Nemzeti Szalon[22]. According to a review published in the 1929 volume of *Magyar Iparművészet* her exhibits were considered "striking"[23]. They were described as the highly

promising attempts of a "very talented young woman, whose gifts will raise her to the foremost rank of our modern ceramists provided that by serious work and perseverance she acquires the necessary qualities for 'arrival'—notably indispensable proficiency in sculpture, draughtsmanship and ceramic technology"[24]. Thus Margit Kovács was one of those fortunate artists who are praised and appreciated from the first moment of their appearance.

The homecoming from Munich was followed by laborious years of study. In her search for various ways of modelling her material, for an individual mode of expression, the young artist showed the feverish energy that was to be one of her characteristics. From the art of the past, and from contemporary art too, she merged into her idiom of forms all that she felt as closest to her own personality, tone and style. At this time life was very hard for her. She rented a small flat where she worked in the kitchen, with her mother acting as her "little apprentice"—not only her mainstay, but also her assistant, friend and manager. Like most Hungarian ceramists of the period she had no kiln in which to bake her pottery.

The politico-social collapse after World War I and the subsequent counter-revolutionary dictatorship of 1919–21 were followed by years of so-called "consolidation", but the general crisis of 1929 affected the already unstable Hungarian economy in a most disastrous way. The plight of artists became desperate. In 1929 the *Magyar Iparművészet* commented as follows on the situation: "Complaints concerning the present sad predicament of Hungarian artist-craftsmen and applied arts generally are understandable, for neither artist-craftsmen nor the applied arts are appreciated by the Hungarian people as might be expected... There are few openings and when there is work to be done professional trained artist-craftsmen are often ignored." Artist-craftsmen, including ceramists, "demand more opportunities for work so that they can make a living and not be compelled to leave the country or accept inferior work in other fields... It must be admitted that progress in the applied arts was halted by the war, and consequently there has been none of the development in applied arts seen in countries which are more advanced culturally. Another reason for this setback in our applied arts is due to the impoverishment of the middle classes. With few exceptions, the most generous and ardent patrons of Hungarian applied arts were not of high rank, nor were they noblemen or church dignitaries, but members of the professions such as teachers, lawyers, physicians; also well-educated merchants, craftsmen and clerks. In fact, these were the classes most affected by the economic collapse, for their reduced circumstances allowed them to buy only the barest necessities, and there was scarcely any money left to spend on applied arts."[25]

In such adverse conditions Margit Kovács, like her talented colleagues, István Gádor, Géza Gorka and many others, had a hard struggle to earn a living. Poor as she was she continued to develop her technical skill, seeking to define her own message and to devise the most adequate means of conveying it.

At what point does an artist begin to feel sure of himself? What is the mysterious borderline beyond which the pupil matures into the master, the moment when tone, rhythm and image become entirely individual? There are artists whose personality emerges quite suddenly; others pass unobserved from a derivative period to a period of individual expression, when the artist's work gives a hint of some future masterpiece. And is there any moment when we can say that the master is no longer a pupil? In the œuvre of Margit Kovács the stages towards maturity can be clearly traced. In fact, after Munich her works were already beginning to reveal something of her own ideas and attitudes as an artist; already it was possible to appreciate the world of forms and motifs which gradually gave her a place among the most famous exponents of the art of glazed pottery in Hungary and indeed Europe. In tone her first attempts were nearer to her inmost being than the more rigid stylized works she made in the thirties, although the later development followed necessarily from existing social and artistic conditions and expectations.

By the thirties Margit Kovács had finally worked out her methods and techniques. Like Hertha Bucher she experimented with composition and theme using tiny clumps of clay, thereby retaining the vivid freshness and emotional content of the moment of conception; in her forms she fused the stylized geometrical Wiener Werkstätte treatment of lines with a sort of orientalism, recalling Persian (Sassanide) looped braids. This geometrical treatment of lines is also frequently to be seen in figural examples of the applied arts in Hungary at that time, for instance, in István Gádor's works, also as ornamentation in the works of artists associated with the architect Lajos Kozma.

As in other European countries, the applied arts of that period were built up of heterogeneous elements and stylistic tendencies. In the interwar period a variety of historical styles were revived. In official quarters there was support for the Neo-Baroque trend, but a wish to revive the earlier styles of the Middle Ages is also evident in the architecture and applied arts of the era (for instance the Roman Catholic Episcopal See and Theological College of Szeged and a number of Roman Catholic Churches). The Hungarian variant of the *art nouveau* was also still a living influence in architecture and the applied arts; and constructivism developed in the circle of Kassák while in the late twenties Neo-Classicism was also cultivated.

By the end of the twenties the picture was becoming even more diversified by the activities of the Bauhaus architects and the artist-craftsmen associated with that movement, also by the work of Lajos Kozma, who exerted a profound influence on modern architecture and interior decoration, as well as by the group of applied artist-craftsmen associated

with him; inspired by contemporary artistic trends (particularly by the Art Deco of Vienna) they interpreted folk traditions in a modern spirit.

Margit Kovács was one of these innovators in the field of applied arts; the works she produced in these years—vessels, ornamental objects, vases, candlesticks, lamps—reveal a familiarity with her material, a more rustic tone and the soft, velvety use of fluid varnish she learned to use in Vienna. The forms she adopted for these works were those commonly used by progressive artist-craftsmen, suited to the requirements of the contemporary style of interior decoration. Her colour schemes can be traced to her Viennese influences, as also her predilection for figural ornamentation learnt from Hertha Bucher. At the 398th Collective Show arranged in the Nemzeti Szalon in June 1928, Margit Kovács exhibited "...black and yellow cups, a blue vase decorated with yellow grapes, a blue vase with figures in relief, candlesticks with blue handles, and a blue dish adorned with motifs in relief". Blue is still one of her favourite colours, its shades ranging from dark tints to the turquoise she most frequently uses, preferably accompanied by a complementary yellow. In this period she still applied a cream-like off-white tin glaze as fluid varnish with coloured, often purple, patches. This varnish, permitted to "run" slightly, created the impression of modern, unfinished shapes and a return to ancient, primitive techniques, thus giving a casual air of individual achievement, rustic in its effect as opposed to perfectly regular factory products. It was in this way, as a result of the experiments carried out by French craftsmen, that Ruskin's theory was incorporated in modern ceramics.

Her frequent use of figures of vigorous loose-limbed animals may also be ascribed to the influence of Hertha Bucher. In this exhibition, Margit Kovács showed four such pieces *(Vase with Stags, Candlestick with Three Animal Figures, Three-branched Candlestick with Two Animals, Duck-shaped Candlestick)*. The principal theme of her mature art, the human figure, was already evident in this early period, usually in relief or moulded in the round *(Blue Vase with Figure Reliefs, Little Man Holding a Fruit Dish, Fluteplayer)*.

The *Three-branched Candlestick with Two Animals* illustrated in the 1929 volume of *Magyar Iparművészet*, though still faithful to the Viennese influence, points to later developments in ornamentation[26], while being closely related to contemporary Hungarian aspirations. The sturdy, racy, hand-formed body of the three-branched candlestick with its fluid glazing was a popular form in Art Deco ornamental pottery. The two stags, both looking backwards, set at different heights between the arched branches of the candlestick, recall, with their intricately stylized, scroll-like, wavy lines, bag-plates from the era of the Hungarian Conquest. These two stags offer the first glimpse of the individual ornamental style to be evolved later by Margit Kovács, who so imaginatively varied the fundamental idea of superimposed animals used in the compositions of the School of Vienna. A variant of this idea, developed along the lines of tectonics, may be found in the animal figures created by István Gádor around 1926. However, following her own leanings in decoration, Margit Kovács, in stylizing her figures, was more influenced by old Hungarian motifs, and also by Persian (Sassanide) ideas of ornamentation. Thus the very same aspirations of style are realized simultaneously in different forms, determined by the individual artist's disposition and temperament.

The most promising work shown by Margit Kovács in this exhibition was a tile, suitable for insertion in a wall, representing a kneeling woman; it is moulded in a simple manner reminiscent of the School of Munich.

Throughout her life, the religious pathos of Karl Killer, her master in Munich, has captivated the imagination of Margit Kovács and provided her with a fruitful heritage. The master's uniquely devout œuvre thus achieved a mysterious after-life in Margit Kovács's own unique experiences, forms and motifs, for she was acutely receptive and sensitive to every impression. These works are the confessions of a repentant soul, for Margit Kovács was also unable to avoid the general trend of the late twenties, conversion. Holy Virgins trembling for the Child, quivering with pain, or transfigured by the glory of motherhood, St. George killing the dragon, apostles and saints—which occur again and again with varying significance in her life-work—reveal that it was not the dictates of religious trend which Margit Kovács followed; it was the human dramas of the Bible that she appreciated and in religious themes she was projecting her own problems and emotional crises. The pupil who looked on Killer as her master surpassed him while little more than a girl. She had more to offer and of a different kind: in the years of the economic crisis which in Hungary assumed disastrous proportions, she was true to her own instincts, those of her own generation, and so found her way back to a forgotten piety, whereas in her later works she aspired to a Baroque splendour and the timeless dignity of Byzantine art. She created for herself a poetic mode of expression with brightly coloured lavish decorations; with nervous, sensitive, undulating, whirling lines; with new rhythm and symbols and with a new mysticism.

The years before 1935, when she held her first exhibition, were a period of continual development towards maturity. From 1929 relief became the keynote, while figures moulded in the round first appeared in her work in the year 1931. This was a time of study and experiment, a ceaseless search for diverse modes of artistic expression, for ways in which she could 'run' glazes, experiments in technique and modelling. A single happy solution did not satisfy her; every chance effect was tested and tried systematically. Various depths of plastic representation were investigated, as also were the contrasting effects of light and shade. Some of her works from this period are imbued with the solemnity of inspiration;

for example *Paradise*, dating from 1929 and related in form elements to the tile *Kneeling Woman*, was one of the principal works of this early period. In the centre of a coloured and varnished relief, reminiscent of Romanesque relics, the devil-headed serpent symbolizing sin twists himself around the apple-tree, while the large-headed figures of Adam and Eve, crouching in the upper branches of the tree, are weighed down by the consciousness of guilt. The composition is crowded; on the left the artist modelled a bird and on the right a stag as motifs symbolizing Paradise.

Another major work of this early period is the equally crowded composition *Cain and Abel* in terracotta relief. In the foreground Cain is seen holding a lamb in his hands while Abel kneels facing him. The power of the rough modelling is enhanced by the absence of glaze; thus the plastic values of the high relief are accentuated more intensively by the effects of light and shade.

The small relief *Jacob's Dream*, dating from 1929, bears the title and date of the work. Jacob is placed in the centre of the composition; the angel with a trumpet on the left provides another reference to the story in the Bible. In the right, a tree indicates the country setting of the story. This is one of a series of terracotta reliefs with religious themes; one of them is inscribed "MARIA" and another relief, also dating from 1929, is called *Mary with Two Hired Mourners*. With these figures of "professional mourners" Margit Kovács introduced a peculiar, frequently recurring motif in her art.

Her works with biblical themes were mostly produced during the thirties. After the war and the suppression of the revolution, religious themes were taken up in Central Europe "as social and psychological symbols". In Hungary it was not only academicians following conservative trends, but progressive painters, too, who turned to religious themes. German artists were foremost in the mystical representation of contemporary reality: thus Beckmann in his *Deposition*, Erich Haeckel in his *Madonna*, Lyonel Feininger in his *Cathedral* used their art to protest against the horrors of war. The theoretical foundations of the trend were laid down by Egon Hoffmann, who set the modern artist the target of "...being, in effect and purpose, a prophet". Among the sources of new art, primitive art is mentioned by the art historians of the age which, together with the sacred art of Orthodox Christianity and the Gothic Era, was thought to serve "... progress towards a future spiritual community"[27]. In Munich, as a girl, Margit Kovács instinctively joined this expressionist tendency and actually remained faithful to its principles when other trends came to prevail after World War II.

Transplanted into Hungarian soil the transcendental and religious aspects of German Expressionism had the effect of turning Margit Kovács to more robust and sober artistic solutions; she relaxed and found calmer forms. Another fundamental feature of expressionist style was the revival of the strange logic and idioms of form found in primitive art; in Margit Kovács's art renewal came about through her response to Hungarian folk art.

In the 1929 volume of *Magyar Iparművészet* Endre Farkas spoke of the new form as follows: "In contemporary art primitive form is a spiritual need; an adherence, as it were, to humanity, the earth, the past. It is a longed-for escape from the frigid beauty of technical perfection. With the passage of time we have lost our sense of contact with the earth; the aeroplane, the radio and the implication of what is yet to come, have made us realize at what speed we leave nature behind us; however, the new, primitive form, still fashioned by the human brain with human love, will prevent the final death of the soul."[28]

When Margit Kovács first began to express herself in her art she listened attentively to the innermost voice of her being. She merely allowed herself to be stimulated by artistic movements, so that she was thus encouraged to express her own world. Her forms became firm and earth-bound, her colours soft, her glazes velvety. In the relationship between theme and form it was the theme which had the dominant role. The art of Margit Kovács developed in a direction quite contrary to that of German Expressionism; the forms typical of the latter were extreme whereas she strove to achieve closed forms. Her work was chiefly distinguished from that of her contemporaries by its emotional content; it was full of passion, revealing even in the modelling the tense excitement of its conception. Her compositions are crowded, with mobile effects of light and shade, in spirit elegiac, exalted, not only when the theme is sacred, but also when she represents, for instance, men at work.

This artificial Golden Age, coupled with Neo-Classicist forms, emerged in the period after World War I all over Europe in both literature and art. However, its forms of manifestation varied widely between individual countries. This was the period when Picasso painted his huge female figures in the manner of antique statues. This spurious Golden Age also had its impact on German Expressionism. In Hungary the trend produced idyllic works and religious allegorical compositions.

The Italian movement Valori plastici, initiated by Chirico and Carrà in the late twenties, was transplanted to Hungarian soil by the Roman School, thus contributing an idyllic pathos to the Hungarian tradition of fine arts.

Genre figures were the principal subjects seen at exhibitions of applied arts. In the years when Margit Kovács was still working out her own style, the chief exponents of the modern applied arts in Hungary were the students of Jaschik's School, particularly István Gádor and Géza Gorka, who made glazed pottery. The Hungarian faience factories, Herend and Zsolnay, stagnated and critics wrote in the press that, "We have seen nothing that satisfies the present artistic requirements of our age, while mere copying of exclusively old patterns suggests that contemporary artist-craftsmen are unable to design good china."[29]

By this time the major change resulting from the constructivist trend had run its course, and now it was Lajos Kassák and his associates who were a source of fruitful inspiration for the arts in Hungary, including the applied arts.

Everywhere members of the avant-garde were trying out new ambitious ideas which became the source of contemporary art. This generation of "isms" made fragmentation absolute and bestowed independence on contributory elements. With the art of Piet Mondrian analysis reached the plastic sign abstraction of the De Stijl group. Yet it was also these same artists of the avant-garde who initiated in the first third of the century a synthesis of the Bauhaus trend with all its implications, thus abandoning the idea of destruction for that of construction. In 1923, as economic conditions became more stable, the De Stijl movement proclaimed: "The period of destruction is over. We have come to the dawn of a new epoch: the epoch of construction."[30] The avant-garde movements in the field of fine arts have scarcely affected form. Nevertheless progressive artists during the last thirty or forty years have transformed our view of the world; artists, architects, poster-artists, designers, industrial designers and artist-craftsmen have all contributed to the reshaping of our environment.

In the field of ceramics avant-garde constructivist features are mainly encountered in the late twenties and early thirties in the works of István Gádor, but also in the forms of Géza Gorka's vessels. In a review of the exhibition arranged by the Society of Applied Arts in 1932[31], the writer commented that some of the pieces shown by István Gádor displayed new features of his art. These simplified lines, both of form and decoration, first appeared in Hungarian applied arts around 1930, simultaneously with a novel stylized treatment of folk motifs.

At this time Margit Kovács was scarcely concerned with avant-garde trends; the simplification of forms to geometrical elements, mainly the potter's cone, appeared only around 1934–35, when she used it, adorned with her individual decorative motifs, for a series of small pieces turned on the potter's wheel.

In the years around 1930 Margit Kovács sought for her peculiar, individual idiom of forms in a number of experiments. Various series of vessels, vases, coffee-sets, candlesticks, reliefs with or without glazing, bear testimony to a fervent search for her own medium of expression; and all the while she was experimenting with different techniques. She also experimented in creating terracotta reliefs, of which one small example, the *Boy at the Potter's Wheel*, may be seen in Szentendre at the entrance to the house now arranged as a museum in which examples of every period of her work are displayed. This work, in high relief, centres on the figure of the potter's apprentice—symbol of the artist. The execution is terse, confined to essentials: above the figure of the apprentice finished vessels are arranged in a row on a shelf. The potter's tools, half-finished jugs, a broom propped against the seat, give the work the atmosphere of a conversation piece; though quite small it has a monumental quality.

One especially characteristic feature of the art of Margit Kovács is the way in which she contrives to incorporate her signature and the date of the work as an organic part of the composition, as on this relief where the letters K. M. serve to provide the foundation for the scene, a ground on which the wheel seems to be supported.

In the early thirties the colour scheme adopted during her years in Vienna was adjusted to her own temperament, and developed into the definitive selection of her own light-hued glazes of turquoise, yellow and white. This is still her most characteristic combination of colours.

First in her series of niche reliefs was that of *St. George* made around 1930. St. George killing the dragon is also a recurring theme in her work. In the art of Margit Kovács St. George symbolizes the idea that by leading a pure and just life man can overcome his difficulties. In these works she was inspired by the rugged idiom of stone sculpture in Romanesque cathedrals. In the proportions of her figures she preserves, sometimes even exaggerates, the medieval form. Her characteristic peasants' heads, sad-featured and big in relation to the body but with relatively long limbs, are modelled sensitively and with understanding, clearly conveying an engaging clumsiness and apparent meekness. In the 1930 Exhibition of the Society of Applied Arts[32] Margit Kovács exhibited vessels shaped like lions or cocks, figures, compositions combining four-branched candlesticks with stags and two-branched candlesticks with foxes. She modelled these animals in the manner of Hertha Bucher, employing the technique of fluid glazes, thus maintaining the traditions of the Wiener Werkstätte.

The first piece of work which she made on commission from the Budapest Municipal Office of Tourism was a high relief, circular in form, on which she used glazes in gay, brilliant colours, the themes being fishing, hunting, livestock-breeding and agriculture. It is strictly closed, symmetrical, and is in four sections. On the *Boy at the Potter's Wheel*, for example, the space round the figure is filled in with delineations of tools, giving the effect of a still-life. On the circular relief the title is modelled along the margin in Latin characters: PISCATUS, VENATUS, PECUARIA, AGRICULTURA, BUDAPEST —K. M., 1931. The inscription is completed with the coat of arms of Budapest.

In most of her works Margit Kovács makes use of the ornamental value of letters of the alphabet. The inscription is inseparable from the work. The type of letters used is in keeping with the emotional content of the composition: peculiar forms are evolved to correspond with a particular period or style. The inscriptions on her early works are in highly plastic modern Roman type and are clearly legible, the form of the characters being slightly simplified.

Critics were alert for new works by Margit Kovács, whose activities they always followed very closely; nearly every year some of her pieces were illustrated in the journal *Magyar Iparművészet*. Before long she acquired a clientele and after 1930 her works were also purchased by the state.

In the early thirties she was chiefly occupied in making pottery for everyday use, for instance coffee services, but later she gave up moulding pieces of this kind. The lion is seen as an ornamental motif in the pieces she made from 1931–32. At this time she was still painting animal motifs on ornamental dishes covered with pink cracked glazing. About 1935 she also abandoned the use of cracked glazing.

It was at the Summer Exhibition of the Society of Applied Arts[33] in 1931 that she exhibited her first pottery figure moulded in the round. Executed in coloured glazing, the little figure is shown sitting with crossed legs and is entitled *Female Figure with Vase*. The plastic modelling is similar to that of *Kneeling Woman*, in its appeal to emotion it is typical of the genre figures so widely favoured during the first thirty years of the present century. The colours are gay and vivid: yellow, off-white, brown.

In the early thirties Margit Kovács became more and more interested in the production of figures. Within a very short period of time she became remarkably proficient in creating glazed plastic figurines. For the most part she modelled genre figures such as the loose-limbed child with a large head, *Little Boy in Nightdress*. The themes of her genre figures were novel: affectionately and meticulously she moulded figures of simple people, mostly young children. The modelling is sensitive, fresh and candid, the tone recalling the naïveté of Romanesque carving. The glazing is greyish-white, a thick, cream-like tin varnish highly characteristic of Margit Kovács's early work.

Further developments in her use of varnish can be followed in the niche-relief entitled *Fishing Boy*, modelled in the year 1932. Here too she studied the light-and-shade effects of glossy glazes in high relief, as also in the niche relief produced in 1933, *Girl Holding on to a Goat*. This high relief, quite small, is richly coloured. The ground of shiny brown intensifies the depth of the relief; it is a charming conversation piece modelled in high relief and full of *joie de vivre*.

In the year 1932 the artist went to Copenhagen, hoping to study under the son of the painter Gauguin, a gifted ceramist and sculptor at the Royal Danish Porcelain Factory. However, as Jean Gauguin did not care for teaching, she worked under J. P. Willumeen for four months. Jean Gauguin, who was also active in the factory at Sèvres, recommended her to go to Paris for a few months. In 1933 Margit Kovács went to Paris where she visited the famous porcelain factory at Sèvres, and showed photographs of her own work to the director, who was sufficiently impressed to give her a contract for several months. It was in Sèvres that she learnt to work with fire-clay *(chamotte)*, the hard and less flexible mass which accustomed her to the moulding of more sweeping, comprehensive forms.

Her first fire-clay figure made at Sèvres, the *Plump-cheeked Girl* (1933–34) reveals innovations both in choice of material and modelling technique. The composition is plain, closed, lacking signs of Viennese bonhomie and expressive moulding. The figure is monumental notwithstanding its small size. In the proportions of the forms—for instance, the relatively big head, loose-limbed hands and feet—there is a link with Margit Kovács's mature works which still retain the dimensions characteristic of her early period. The style of the *Plump-cheeked Girl* was resumed on a more elevated plane in the late fifties.

In Paris Margit Kovács was chiefly fascinated by Gothic art which noticeably influenced her work at this time. The graceful delicate figure of the *Girl Looking into the Mirror* is strongly modelled and elongated like those of saints in Gothic cathedrals. The surface seems to vibrate, the traces of modelling are accentuated by the thick, greyish-white adherent glaze and the darker shadows in the indentations. The *Girl Looking into the Mirror* was followed by the upward gazing *Little Girl* with braids and a tip-tilted nose (1933–34) and by the big, almost life-size *Young Apprentice* modelled in the round about 1934. These genre figures are characterized by the intimacy of tone which Margit Kovács employs to depict work, thus emphasizing the serene frame of mind which accompanies absorption in quiet creative activity.

During the years preceding 1945 the *Young Apprentice* was followed by a series of delightful conversation pieces and compositions on biblical themes; of these, the elongated figure of the *Modest Virgin* (approximately 1935) and *Mother with Her Child* (1935) will find a lasting place in the history of Hungarian glazed pottery.

After returning from Sèvres, Margit Kovács began to prepare for a large one-man exhibition. She turned from the composition of more comprehensive forms and indulged her liking for ornamentation, relying partly on the rich heritage of decorative design in the Hungarian manner, much in vogue at the time, partly on motifs used by Byzantine goldsmiths.

Her turning towards folk tradition and her search for a national style is the triumph of romanticism. At the time it first emerged, it served not only to foster patriotism, but also to advance Hungarian industry. The National Association for the Protection of Industry, under the patronage of Lajos Kossuth (1844–47), encouraged industrial development under the Monarchy as did its successor the Industrial Association. They inspired craftsmen in the field of applied arts to produce pieces of national character. However, in those years the treasures of Hungarian folk art were still not widely known. It was not until the second half of the nineteenth century that Hungarian ethnographers began to make serious collections. In the field of applied arts it was the cultural and industrial policy of the state to support all attempts to formulate a Hungarian style. "...there should be a resurgence of the Hungarian style"[34]. The Industrial Exhibition in 1885 and, even more, the Hungarian village shown at the Millennium Exhibition of 1896, gave a powerful impetus to everyone engaged in formulating the national style.

Certain peculiarities of the applied arts of the Hungarian *art nouveau* are attributable to the new interpretation of national romanticism in which the motifs of every Hungarian region were fused. The eminent Hungarian architects of the age, particularly Ödön Lechner, by using majolica of Zsolnay, Pécs and oriental—chiefly Indian—ornamental elements, created the colourful, romantic and eclectic style seen in Lechner's masterpieces, the Museum of Applied Arts in Budapest and the Town Hall of Kecskemét.

Ödön Lechner strove consciously to develop a national style. He believed that "... the Hungarian people does in fact have an identifiable national Hungarian style; well-trained eyes will soon find the typical features. In the narrow circle of those who seek to satisfy their artistic needs, an idiom of forms has been developed and preserved to this very day. We must seek the language of this popular Hungarian style, just as we have learnt that of the Greek popular style. We must invent its rules, become absorbed in its peculiar spirit, in order to transfer as cultured beings the spirit of the forms into more ambitious, more advanced, even monumental, architectural endeavours. And thence to other arts."[35]

The colony of artists living in Gödöllő in 1902 also had as its aim the development of a modern national style. Using Hungarian ornamental elements these artists sought to fulfil the aims of English *art nouveau* craftsmen in the field of applied arts. The twentieth-century renaissance of Hungarian music also had its origins in the study of Hungarian folk music. As Bartók wrote, "...peasant music, entirely unknown until then, provided an invaluable impetus to those who were beginning to reject conventions"[36]; "who, to put it more precisely, were working towards a 'renewal' "[37]. And Kodály declared, "The Hungarian folk song is not merely the echo of present-day rural life, but also the mirror of the whole Hungarian soul. For centuries every rivulet of Hungarian life flowed into it as into a large cistern which has retained the residue of every mental experience of the Hungarian people, from its earliest beginnings, for there can be no doubt that the Hungarian song and the Hungarian language are of the same age."[38]

It the late twenties this endeavour to create a national style was again revived in the field of fine arts; it was also supported officially by the administration which approved of the unrealistic, chauvinistic ideology of the national mythology. However, in the works of the best architects, craftsmen and artists of the period, aspiration to a national character was accompanied by laborious research and the collection and classification of Hungarian ornamental motifs. István Groh's "Hungarian Ornamental Art" and "New Hungarian Decorations", published in 1929, stimulated research, which continued with increasing enthusiasm until the year 1944. As the country tended more and more towards fascism, it became increasingly reactionary. When opening the First Hungarian Exhibition of Glazed Pottery in 1942 the Minister of Industry said: "Hungarian industry and art cannot be other than Hungarian... To enhance and develop this spirit is a primary task. Pottery is history formed in Hungarian soil..."[39]. "Today the task of the Hungarian ceramist is to bring Hungarian glazed pottery into every house, reverence for the past into every Hungarian soul, his adoration of ancient forms, colours, relics; and proclaim that Hungarian fate bears testimony to our history of a thousand years."[40]

From the year 1874 it was the Zsolnay factory of Pécs that produced ceramics in which a deliberately nationalistic style is discernible. In the wake of these pioneering activities, István Gádor, together with Géza Gorka and Margit Kovács, created the type of modern Hungarian glazed pottery in which folk elements are employed. In the work of all three artists there was a sincere attempt to define a national style in the manner of other applied arts of the period. In this they were significantly encouraged by the reality of the twenties. The tense atmosphere of those days also contributed to a fundamentally progressive, and to some extent left-wing, movement in the thirties among Hungarian populist writers; another influence was the research being undertaken by Bartók and Kodály in music. It was in the late twenties that István Gádor turned for inspiration to folk art. His tiles with scenes from village life are based on his own observations of the Hungarian people's way of life and their favourite forms of ornamentation. Preserving the essence of characteristic features of Hungarian folk costumes he fashioned decorations which, however, he executed only in one-plane representation.

The other leading personality of modern Hungarian ceramics, Géza Gorka, had received his original training from a village potter, Balázs Badár of Mezőtúr, and after the conclusion of his studies abroad, in 1922 he turned once more to the study of folk craft. It was not only contemporary folk pottery in which he was interested, but also old techniques, shapes and ornamentation; he devoted much of his time to learning about Haban pottery which clearly influenced the forms and decorations he developed for his own vessels. In his style, expressed in modern forms and glazes, there is a synthesis of the colours and motifs of popular art and Haban pottery.

From the very beginning Margit Kovács was attracted by Hungarian wood carving and honey-cake forms. Popular ornamentation—flowers, birds, fishes and figures—and its innumerable variations gave a fresh stimulus to her imagination. While transforming typical elements, she retained the structure, but in a different grouping and with the use of richer, more curvilinear design.

The first works inspired by folk motifs were flasks, vases and a few figurines[41]. The shape of the vases was plain, recalling forms of folk art. They were adorned with flowers or birds, the contours being grooved, or moulded from rolls of clay.

On a jug-shaped candlestick a peacock is painted with outspread tail. In the ornamentation of flat, round Hungarian flasks, motifs alien to Hungarian folk art also appear; this is characteristic of the work of Margit Kovács, who for instance much favours the stylized lion. On the lion's head there is usually a crown and, as in other compositions by Margit Kovács inspired by medieval stone sculpture and miniatures, a bushy tail curves in an arch over his back, filling the whole surface; the crown gives the appearance of a spray of blossoming branches. On another flask a highwayman in lace-trimmed coat and a feathery grass in his cap is resting on the ground, holding his rifle in his lap. From the very beginning of her interest in folk art Margit Kovács transformed the elements. She rejects the original stiffness and symmetry and arranges the elements of the motifs in a modern, asymmetrical rhythm. From wood carvings she learnt the technique, the constructive devices and the necessity for concentration, all of which she used to advantage. She retains symmetry, but stiffness is overcome by tiny alterations. Folk art releases her proneness to improvisation, her responsiveness to playful impulses, stimulating her to give adequate expression to her thoughts and feelings.

Her first figures moulded in the round, representing girls wearing folk costumes, striding grotesquely in their long, lace-trimmed skirts, the naive form of the heads remotely influenced by African sculpture, have an awkwardness that has not yet been refined by grace. The animal figures formed in the round, especially the recumbent bulls and donkeys with their oversized heads and clumsy postures are, however, unmistakably worthy of her signature. On a dumpy two-eared vase we find a pigeon with outspread wings, a motif which was to be much favoured by Margit Kovács in her works after the year 1945.

Her fanciful imagination fed not only on Hungarian folk art, but also on the ornamental wealth of Byzantine and medieval Persian motifs. She was inspired by Byzantine icons to develop the ornamental technique still characteristic of her mural pictures and figures. By adorning the haloes of her saints, the crowns of her kings and the hems of their splendid garments, with blue, yellow and crimson spots of glossy glaze, she hoped to indicate the splendour of the sparkling precious stones used on icons.

Some of Margit Kovács's work found a place in every exhibition of the applied arts; and with every showing her work was more widely appreciated. In 1933 she was awarded a silver medal for her exhibit at the Fourth Triennale of Milan, thus winning international recognition at an early age.

An exhibition of her collected works in 1935 marked the end of her first period, a period of study and orientation. She had by now found her themes and learnt to wield her tools. She had reverted to the simplicity of the potter's wheel and using it in her own unique way she became capable of producing major works that could be placed somewhere between the fine and applied arts. Turning the wheel, painting with clay-glaze, engobe work, the use of lead and heavy zinc, so-called opaque varnishes, engraving—what she called "scraping"—on clay as hard as leather[42] and various kinds of modelling—all the simple techniques of the village potter were reinterpreted in the hands of Margit Kovács. Reviewing the exhibition of 1935 Hungarian critics pronounced that "this young woman, an excellently trained potter, is one of our finest modern ceramists..."[43]

Her coloured ceramic pictures were at the time said to be "...on the verge between painting and modelling... It is enchanting to see with what flair and taste she imitates the styles of long past epochs, for instance that of the primitive reliefs of the Romanesque Era or of folk pottery. Every one of her works is an artistic achievement", concluded the critic[44].

Most of her works have religious themes, and biblical scenes are frequently found on her vessels.

Annunciation I, made in 1935, is a small, turquoise-glazed tile framed with open-work in which the style of Gothic reliefs is blended with the floral ornamentation and technical devices found in Hungarian wood carvings. Critics noted the artistic values of her figurines, emphasizing that "she is noteworthy as a sculptor, a fact which is demonstrated particularly in a few small figures in which the magnificently life-like motion fully conforms with the sculptural style"[45].

From 1920 onwards, religious and historical themes began to appear more frequently in Hungarian art. To meet the kind of interest that was stimulating Neo-Classicist historical mural painting, Margit Kovács attempted to develop a monumental style of ceramic art. With her own gaiety and charm she first fused the brightly-coloured decorative motifs of Gothic and Persian miniatures and Byzantine mosaics with the motifs used by Lajos Kozma and his associates —motifs reminiscent of Hungarian Baroque and carried out by the techniques employed by shepherds in their carvings, the mood and content being indicated by the theme. In the design, and in the elaboration of the faces and hands, there is a contemporary sensitivity which sometimes permits caricature, thus safeguarding the work from sentimentalism.

After the exhibition of 1935 Margit Kovács developed a style that was both monumental and decorative. She continued her series of highly plastic niche-reliefs with that of the small *St. Florian* modelled in 1935 for the house of Gyula Kaesz in Szentendre.

The building industry, everywhere revived during the temporary boom of the thirties, brought ever more commissions to artists. Margit Kovács's talent for the decorative and her rich gift for the narrative found a new outlet when she was commissioned to create architectural ceramics. These usually took the form of small reliefs or mural pictures for mounting in their finished form on buildings or in the vestibules of apartment houses in Budapest; not infrequently she was asked to decorate fireplaces. This work continued to absorb her from the year 1932 to 1945, some of her most important commissions being obtained from the Roman Catholic Church.

In the mural dating from 1937 entitled *The History of the Mail Service*[46], a work highly characteristic of this period, both in its conception and manner of composition, the figures are placed one over the other, as if cut out. The tiny genre pieces are connected by rhythm and the emotional content expressed by movement. Perspective is solved by the perpendicular position of the series of superimposed scenes, as in Persian miniatures or Egyptian frescoes. Thus representation is entirely on one plane. The mingling of various elements suggests the technique of montage favoured in avantgarde trends. For instance, the long-robed angel, Byzantine in effect, flying in the direction of the telegraph-pole above the aeroplane, creates a quite grotesque impression.

In another mural from 1937, *Let's Respect Women!*[47], the peculiar atmosphere is created by the merging of Gothic miniature figures and a wealth of Hungarian motifs taken from the ornamental carvings of shepherds.

The work made for the Budapest Hall of the Paris World Exhibition in 1937, and awarded a Certificate of Distinction, was painted in the same style. This was a mural created in coloured and glazed terracotta, the theme indicated by the title *Budapest, the Queen of the Danube*. The crowned female figure occupying the centre of this U-shaped, exceedingly ornamental picture personifies Budapest; other figures surrounding her symbolize the crafts and sciences, while in the two upright side sections are representations of well-known views of the historic city.

Murals conceived in the Byzantine style are more closely knit in composition and more monumental in tone, for instance the picture of *Mark and Luke* dating from the year 1938. The coloured square tiles of the floor stand out against the dark background which is also a foil for the pale shimmering garments and haloes of the two apostles standing facing each other. It was in this work that Margit Kovács first experimented with cement embedding in an attempt to heighten the contrast between the surfaces of materials of varying texture, and to sharpen the decorative effect. These pictures give something of the effect of a fresco; the aim is monumentality and the series illustrates the experimental stage in the artist's development in the exacting craft of mural ceramics. Her individuality is revealed in her very first prototypes, for at this time no other artist was using Byzantine art as a source of inspiration.

The Last Supper, made in the year 1938, long and rectangular in shape, and embedded in cast stone, is in a filleted ornamental frame. The style of representation harmonizes wonderfully with the strictly symmetrical composition; the execution is quite different from that of the detailed mosaic-like *Budapest, the Queen of the Danube*. The colours are dark, the picture being divided into four fields by the horizontal planes of the table and seats. The largest, uppermost field is emphasized by a tympanum below which are the seated figures of Jesus and the apostles Andrew and John. Four disciples form the lower row. On the table, symbolizing the Lord's supper, are the geometrically simplified forms of a cup, bread and fish. Within the three closed angles of the tympanum, heads of seraphim, Byzantine in style, have been placed by the artist as space-filling elements. The effect is solemn, almost grim. However, the moulding of the faces is modern, in both proportion and form characteristic of the types created by Margit Kovács. Critics noted this peculiar style: "The artist has evolved a style of her own, a blend of Byzantine and primitive features." They wrote of her works as "seething, questing...", and she is referred to as "... one of the most promising of Hungarian ceramists"[48].

Although all her works in the Byzantine style are cherished as superb examples of modern Hungarian ceramics, it is a nature piece dating from 1938, *Annunciation II*, which has a special charm for us because of its quality of devout tenderness. The fragile figure of Mary is depicted enthroned and wearing splendid Byzantine robes as she bows gently to greet the angelic messenger kneeling in homage. The purity and calligraphic quality of the design is enhanced by being cut into clay. The garments of the Virgin are lavishly decorated in Margit Kovács's customary style, the dotted, latticed edges brilliantly glazed and introducing the stylized, brightly coloured tulips in the Hungarian convention. The faces, with their thin eyebrows, casually drawn mouths, deep-set, far-gazing eyes, are nervous, sensitive, modern. In their proportions the figures conform to the Gothic pattern; long, attenuated ethereal figures through which the artist conveys and stresses the religious aspect of the theme. For the most part she applied mat, engobe colours, somewhat dimmed for the faces, and the most striking parts of the ornamentation are set off by the use of white. The folds of the garments are shaded with engobe painting or engraved.

Annunciation II frankly proclaimed her increasing interest in decorative elements of Hungarian origin. In a review written in 1937 Sándor Mihalik commented, "Attempts to achieve a Hungarian style are rarely discernible"[49], although the mural painted in 1937 and inspired by the Hungarian folk song *Lace-Bird* disclosed such a trend in the artist's work. However, works from the year 1938—both mural pictures and pieces moulded in the round—show how her art had become increasingly dominated by Hungarian elements.

The huge *Ornamental Stove* made for the First National Exhibition of Applied Arts in 1938 demonstrates this Hungarian character only in the choice of theme. This stove, conceived in the manner of the famous ornamental stoves of the Middle Ages, was much praised, winning the gold medal of the capital, Budapest, and the silver medal of the Sixth Triennale of Milan in 1939 where it found a buyer. The stove, with its terracotta base and engraved contour design in engobe colouring, was built of tiles adorned with figures. For her themes Margit Kovács turned to Hungarian history. Inspired by medieval illuminated manuscripts and Persian miniatures, she represented important episodes of history in a style that is at once epic and detailed. On this stove Margit Kovács made full use of her vast store of knowledge. Notwithstanding the profusion of detail, often highly dramatic, the work as a whole is harmonious, while niche-reliefs and statues in the round reveal the virtuosity of her plastic technique.

In December 1938, her works were exhibited together with those of Lajos Erdős and István Pekáry at the Tamás Gallery in Budapest. She was much praised as the Hungarian ceramist with "the most intriguing talent" and it was said that her religious pieces were imbued with the piety that pervades works by old masters. Her figure of St. George and her icon in the Byzantine style were said to be "exceedingly characteristic of this highly gifted artist whose remarkable works we saw at the Exhibition of Applied Arts—the painted glazed tile stove with miniatures"[50]. The critic of *Esti Kurír* considered Margit Kovács to be the leading personality in the art of ceramics. "The decorative elements of her pitchers and bowls express a talent that is both individual and original."[51]

In the late thirties her interest was captured again by pieces moulded in the round. The *Flute-player*, modelled in 1936, is her only work executed also in terracotta.

The first pieces of series of figures, known as the "Hungarian Tanagras", varying greatly in type, date from this period. In these relatively small but highly exacting figures of glazed pottery Margit Kovács continued to synthetize the traditional and the modern, one of the most remarkable being the *Pound-cake Madonna*, which was inspired by a Baroque icon of Mariazell.

It was not only on her figures in the round and her mural pictures that Margit Kovács worked for this effect but also on her vessels. A round mirror-frame with two candlesticks signed "*Vanitatum Vanitas* 1936 KM." is an outstanding piece of functional glazed pottery. During this period, inspired by folk tales, she developed peculiar forms for dishes and jugs on which she gave new expression to Hungarian folk songs. The *Large Pitcher* of 1938, with engraved decoration in engobe colours, represents three moments in the act of drinking. Frequently her vessels are abundantly decorated within and without; she prefers complex, virtuose moulded figures: black engobe pitchers with the animal shapes personifying the evangelists *Matthew, Mark, Luke* and *John*, and the *Vase with Archer*. Her grey engobe pigeon was turned on the wheel, a figure in the round completed in the fifties and a plastic precursor of figures composed of balls.

The most monumental of her architectural ceramics created before 1945 is *The Entrance of St. Imre's Church at Győr*, produced in 1939–40. The entrance was accentuated by the architect in Bauhaus style and Margit Kovács's mural picture was placed there. In the section above the entrance the artist represented the symbols of faith, hope and love; over each front pillar an angel was modelled with outspread wings; while for the columns she created symbols of the virtues Wisdom, Justice, Strength and Moderation in simplified Byzantine inspired shape.

From the mid-thirties onwards, Margit Kovács made es increasing number of works for export. When interviewed in 1936 she spoke of having been commissioned to make articles for everyday use and ornamental pieces for America.[52] By now she was financially secure, and was therefore able to have a kiln constructed for her own use. From this time on, she was in a position to devote herself wholly to her work. Since then she has satisfied a wide demand from many quarters for her extraordinarily popular small and toy-like ornamental pieces "of primitive forms painted in delicate colours"[53]: little horses, simplified tree-trunks, cone-shaped Byzantine saints, crowned and gorgeously robed, also figures of angels which in some cases have a practical use as candlesticks or vases.

A second, extremely successful exhibition of her collected works was held in 1942. This constituted a summary of her creative activity and development from the year 1935. Critics were unanimous in emphasizing the "individual timbre" of her art, "all playful stylization"[54], and were particularly enthusiastic about the "decorations of churches". Of her one-plane ornamentation it was said that, "the play of lines is of lace-like delicacy". Critics commented on the fact that "moulding, painting, embroidery and goldsmith's work are produced simultaneously"[55] and that "the essence of her art is serene playfulness and ingenuity"[56]. Murals in Byzantine style were referred to as "frescoes come to life"[57]. There was particular praise for the *Adoration of the Magi* (1942), in which the technique employed for *Annunciation II* was further elaborated—the combination of engobe painting and tin glazes. *Bethlehem*, turned on the wheel, is remarkable for its intimate atmosphere, charm, and freedom from conventional features. In most instances pieces in the Byzantine style are burnt in dark brown clinker (vitrified brick). Economically applied yellow-white, crimson spots of glaze, turquoise or white characters and ornamental motifs stand out, warm and glowing, against the dark background. The decorative effect of the pictures is enhanced by contrasting colours—dark-brown and white, and surfaces—some dull, others glossy. This technique was also tried on clinker, for instance in the tondi of the *Apostles Peter and Paul*, and in *St. Peter* and *Angel-column*.

Again and again Margit Kovács sought to express her gifts by creating icons of the Holy Virgin for shrines at places of pilgrimage. Her *Virgin and Child*, Mary wearing a crown with little Jesus in robes resting in her arms, was created in the Byzantine style on a clinker base; the garments are adorned with the elaborate and stylized, foliated scroll-like design so popular in bobbin lace and the work is clearly a late lyrical descendant of sombre Byzantine icons (1938–42).

Rather like a tree-trunk, elongated in the Gothic style and burnt to a dark colour, the clinker figure of *The Good Shepherd* (1942) is a memorable expression of the faith that expects miracles.

Typically Hungarian forms and types of ornamentation were the source of her inspiration when she came to depict folk tales. It was in the early forties that she began to explore folklore and the works she made as a result of this interest brought her ever greater popularity. Her modelling became more lively and the same quality may be seen in her moulded or painted mural pictures.

In this field, too, Margit Kovács found her individual tone only by experiment. The famous aesthete, Sándor Mihalik, characterized the individual traits of her art in these words: "The dream world of the Arabian Nights, so full of colour, woven from threads of gold and silver and glittering with precious stones, is brought to life in the creative hands of this woman. Every piece tells its own tale of the rich, fanciful world of a poet... her design is as sincere and unsophisticated as the naive work of medieval artists"[58].

Sleeping Beauty (1942) illustrates her new inspiration: the form is no longer based on her appreciation of medieval miniatures, it is a reassessment of popular tradition.

It was also in 1942 that she produced the large bas-relief *Fishing, Hunting* in which she achieves perspective for the figures by the brilliance of the composition. Later she employed a similar solution in her painted murals. To preserve the one-plane character while creating an illusion of spatial depth, she superimposed one form over another. Figures with large heads, like those found on icons, express the fabulous nature of the theme, a method of composition designed to create the dreamlike reality of folklore.

In the terracotta relief *May God Grant Wine, Wheat and Peace* (1942) the artist experiments with yet another technique, this time similar to that used in ivory carving. Strongly contoured to stand out against a hollowed background, the three female figures with flat crowns and antique garments, holding grapes and ears of corn, were carved before the firing. In contrast to her earlier colour schemes, it is the shining yellowish bone-coloured glaze which is dominant in this work, in which she also used vivid combinations of white, tomato-red and green. The types of faces derive from a new conception of the forms of Byzantine icons. Characteristic features are the high, strongly arched, shaded, expressive eyebrows, long noses, thick sensual eyelids, large, sad, yearning eyes and full, erotic mouths that are almost grotesque.

Increasingly powerful representations of faces, approaching portrayal, indicated a new phase in the career of Margit Kovács. Instead of types she began to study individuals. In the fifties, however, she gave up portraits and returned to types: thus she moved from the general to the individual, from the individual to the general.

Her figurines, in size around 40 cm, painted in adobe and decorated with coloured glazes, are products of Margit

Kovács's marked capacity for keen observation, her delight in living and her sense of humour. They are unmistakable, full of character in a world of their own. The first example of a type that was to recur later was *Salome* (c. 1943–44), a slender figure in a flowery tomato-red gown that calls to mind the *Sleeping Beauty*. Salome's face reveals depths of malice and cruelty as she regards with astonishment John the Baptist's head resting on the platter in her hands.

The series of genre figures representing children was continued with *Girl Picking Flowers* (1938), *Little Girl with Doll II* (1942–43) and others. In most of the figures of the series "Old Album of Photographs" the facial expressions are grotesque, being intended to parody the petty bourgeoisie (e.g. *Woman with Mirror*). *Beau* is one of the most amusing of these, a figure attired in grotesquely clumsy, Sunday-best clothes.

As fascism began to grip the country and conditions deteriorated, the sensation of imminent physical and mental danger stimulated artists to use biblical themes once again. In February 1944, Margit Kovács created holy-water basins, angels and various works with religious themes.[59] A niche-relief (1944) represents the archangel *St. Michael* slaying the dragon with his sword, St. Michael mounted, the dragon rearing and twisting at the feet of his horse. The picture symbolizes protest against the horrors of war and at the same time faith in the victory of truth and valour. A sequel to this masterly composition was to appear in the fifties. The excellently characterized face, with all the individuality of a portrait, brings the execution of St. Michael near to that of *Salome*.

The great reversal of fortunes in Hungarian history in 1945 changed the trend of Margit Kovács's art. At first all creative activity was badly hampered by inflation and lack of raw materials. But Margit Kovács's intention, as she told a journalist in 1945, was to take up creative work as soon as she had wood to heat her kiln.[60]

She made every endeavour to take part in the new way of life and accepted her share of the cares of the community. As early as in 1945 she arranged an exhibition in her studio, saying, "...Liberation has made men conscious of many things—past errors, new ideas and relationships. This atmosphere has brought me closer to the present in which there is so much frankness." Her mood was one of optimism. "These two words, historical change, mean so many truly grand things today—freedom, welfare, culture... This form of art, ceramics, serves ornamentation, beauty, joy. Its aim can only be, and has to be, to express good cheer and joy within the possibilities of the medium."[61]

However, the period of inhumanity and horror was slow to fade from her mind. The figures of professional mourners (*Two Mourners*, c. 1944) were forged out of her memories of war. These elongated figures express drama and pain. The tear-stained faces, the bewildered and desolate stance, the hands clutching mourners' kerchiefs, express helplessness.

Other works based on biblical themes were *Man with Lamb*, completed in 1944–45, the King bearded and wearing a coronet, holding in his hands a lamb turning to the left; *The Admirable Catch;* and *St. Luke*, a mural (1948). These works show the gradual looming of inner tension. The figure of *Corpus*, also moulded in 1948, indicated a transformation of strictly Byzantine forms.

Her figures turned on the wheel became larger, their gestures and attitudes more animated and complex. The artist produced a variety of figures in which she experimented with new methods of modelling, technical solutions and the arrangement of the figures—contrapposto, seated, bending and in pairs. Gradually the colour schemes, too, became brighter and details were again allotted a more prominent role.

The first signs of a new stage in her art appeared sometime after the Liberation in 1945. Her witty parodies of the *fin de siècle* petty bourgeois class were continued in the series in clay *Old Album of Photographs: Gazing Little Girl* (1948), *Theresa* (1947–48)—a splendid rendering of the awkward village girl dressed up for Sunday Mass, *Nosy Girls* (1948), the affected *Lady* (1949), the grotesque and clumsy *Proposal* also from 1948, *Girl with Chinese Eyes* (1948) and *Lady Donning Her Glove* (1949). The decorative treatment is a further development of the techniques devised for *Pound-cake Madonna*. In moulding heads turned on the wheel Margit Kovács made a unique contribution to her art. On the turned, spherical form the eyes are indicated by engraving and painting. The small, usually tip-tilted nose and the full mouth are put on with blobs of clay, while the hair is also fashioned by engraving and painting. Particular care is devoted to the modelling of realistic, very expressive hands. These hands are in strong contrast to the heads which are only types, and with the abstract shape of the figures akin to those produced in peasant art.

Her moulded figures, usually representing children, for instance *Little Girl Drinking* (1947), *Little Girl*, a child clasping her hands in prayer (1948), *Gazing Little Girl* from the same year and *Children at the Puppet Show* (1950), retained the idiom of form used in the genre pieces prior to 1945.

Deliberate portrait-like representations are extremely rare in the work of Margit Kovács. In 1948 she modelled a portrait of her mother *(My Mother)* which she cast in bronze in 1951. It is a portrait of an old woman with a thoughtful, wise face, smiling as she rests her head on both hands. In this work the artist portrayed the woman who not only gave her life but also remained her faithful, helpful companion in every vicissitude of her career.

The year 1948 marks a new period in her art. After the exhibition summarizing her achievements in the 1940s she was now ready to initiate the subsequent period, uniformly gay and serene in its colouring, which brought her to the zenith of her powers. For her creative activity the Hungarian

People's Republic awarded her the Kossuth Prize, distributed for the first time in that year.

After the exhibition, the formerly diverse styles of her art merged into unity and developed in the direction of monumentality. Everyday themes dominated her work and religious subjects were temporarily abandoned.

In her works dating from this period Hungarian folk art was practically her only source of inspiration as regards form. It was principally ornamental elements that she borrowed, using them in her own, novel way. Memories of her childhood welled up like the eruption of a subterranean stream as she created marketwomen, village girls, women cutting bread, ploughmen, girls scanning the sky for rain and picking flowers, old gamekeepers and fishermen, old women weeping and mourning, wedding- and harvest-groups. On her vessels the colouring is also more vivid in these years, with tomato-red predominating.

The economic and social restructuring of the country during the years following World War II afforded more and wider opportunities, hitherto unimaginable, to practitioners in both the fine and applied arts. Whole residential districts were built and there were at the same time ambitious schemes for state factories and offices. These building projects and also higher living standards brought plenty of commissions for ceramists. In her speech of thanks after receiving the Kossuth Prize Margit Kovács declared, "We have been given more than we ever dared to hope for. Commissions provide not only for artistic freedom, but also financial and creative independence."[62]

The first task of István Gádor, Géza Gorka and Margit Kovács was to satisfy the increased demand. The creative activities of these three artists, whose work was so different in both conception and execution, and who differed from each other in their artistic outlook, nevertheless shared one important characteristic: all made use of their rich heritage of Hungarian decorative traditions, forms and patterns, which they used to create highly individual works of the highest standard. According to György Domanovszky, "... everybody else could play only a subordinate role"[63].

These were the happiest years in Margit Kovács's life. For a brief moment of history the needs of society coincided with the availability of creative talents capable of supplying almost everything asked of them. Margit Kovács was also aware of her exceptional position. "I am glad to have lived to this age when the artist can really work for the masses. I can think of no greater satisfaction than to see my works on public buildings, at underground stations or schools... this is the true aim."[64]

For a period of more than a decade Margit Kovács was occupied in producing large and animated terracotta or glazed works, painted or adorned with patterns, for the decoration of walls. At each one of her numerous exhibitions at home and abroad she was more highly praised than before.

As a result of the official attitude to art during the 1950s artists were encouraged to evolve an idiom of form that was at once realistic and fused with folk traditions. To ceramists this was no alien notion. On the contrary, at the beginning they saw in it a chance to develop in new directions; it was only later, in the years after 1952, that it led to schematism, a disregard for the function of objects, and mere copying of traditional popular motifs. The policy was expounded in the *Szabad Nép* in an account of the First Exhibition of Applied Arts, 1952: "...We will break down the dividing wall between professional and popular art."[65]

At first the art of Margit Kovács benefited from the change: "From the utilization of the liberated charm, beauty and lovely security of the new movements, we received tasks so magnificent that we cannot do justice to them, unless we recognize all new realities, allowing our blood to absorb them, so that we are imbued with a new sense of beauty and joy."[66]

However, the official policy was to call upon artists to accomplish short-term projects: to take part in a narrow educational programme that would have been better undertaken by publicists. Artists were told that their work should be a medium for conditioning the mind. This had a harmful effect. In fact, art was incapable of coping with the social tasks demanded of it. Moreover, those responsible for the state policy in regard to art did not set themselves the task of reforming the taste of the masses by carefully considered, patient educational work; rather they set out to simplify the idiom of form in art, with the idea of making it "easily intelligible". So-called "style democratism" also required of the idiom of form that it should have an external "similarity" of theme in the manner of the realistic works of the nineteenth century. There was disapproval for any attempt to establish clarity through "misinterpretation" of the role of tradition, which resulted in the empty imitation of folk motifs in applied arts... "In the applied arts (textiles, ceramics), where folk art motifs were used for decoration, the creation of a unity between socialist content and nationalistic form was seen. What is more, motifs of folk costume, for instance, were hailed in paintings as the manifestation of the popular character of art. The general development of decorative style, in the applied arts and in the creation of forms, was required to influence and condition the mind, no less than painting, sculpture and graphic art."[67]

As with so many other notable exponents of the fine and applied arts in those years, the difficulties encountered by Margit Kovács stemmed from the tension between this approach to socialist-realist representation and her own disposition, especially in regard to decorative effects and stylization. Her second major commission after the Liberation in 1945 was *May First*, *Detail of a Mural* and the *Map of Hungary* composed of 800 tiles to cover the main wall of the frontier station Hegyeshalom. This is described, very characteristically of the spirit of the period, in *Építés–Építészet*

(Building–Architecture No. 5, 1950): "The treasures of the Hungarian soil, the multitude of curative spas, noteworthy industrial and agricultural centres, the characteristic sights of towns, are all shown on the map of the Hungarian People's Republic." To the left above is "... a peasant woman in Hungarian costume and a worker, holding flowers and bread in their hands, acting as spokesmen for the Hungarian People, greet with a 'Salve' visitors to the country. Budapest is indicated by the Fishermen's Bastion and the Chain Bridge, while the Liberation Monument rises beyond the borders of the country, its sheer size and weight conveying the significance of Liberation. The mermaid rising from Lake Balaton holds a heart, at Hévíz a patient throws away his crutches; smoking factory chimneys, mines, furnaces indicate centres of industry. In the Tisza region a girl is shown driving a tractor and a navvy working on the Danube–Tisza canal. These figures bring to life the new physical and spiritual profile of the rapidly changing nation. At Eger a bleeding bull calls to mind the famous red wine of the region; the upside-down church over the sweep-well of Hortobágy signifies the *fata morgana;* Lajos Kossuth addressing the crowd before the Great Church of Debrecen symbolizes freedom. In the representation of the Ják Church and the monumental Iron Works of Győr memories of the past are associated with the realities of the present and the remaining small spaces are generously filled in with flowers. The entire scene is bathed in the serene rays of the sun which sheds a gentle glow over the countryside and on the young men and women singing and marching with banners aloft..."[68]

The map commissioned for the South Railway Station of Budapest in 1950 was composed in a similar spirit. In both maps the characteristic features of various regions are represented in a way that is artistically and technically superior to that of the mosaic-like technique employed in *Budapest, Queen of the Danube* which was executed before 1945.

Glazed pottery embedded in cement was one of her individual technical solutions; this type of work was a logical development of her previous pictures embedded in cast stone. Margit Kovács made a series of experiments to discover the latent possibilities in brick, tile and cement. These pottery murals are actually cut out of a plate of clay as hard as leather and fixed in another material. The composition is engraved in these pieces of clay, tiny reliefs being added for richer ornamentation, which procedure is followed by painting in engobe and covering with glazes. Then the piece is twice fired. The compositions embedded in cement and her pictures in tiles are extremely suitable for the external decoration of buildings. In the fifties they soon became acceptable types of surface decoration for big public buildings.

Am I not Pretty? executed by the same technique in 1951, and representing a young peasant woman clad in national costume, with her mother, is a characteristic work of the period. This figure was developed further in 1953 in *Dressing the Bride* which represents a Matyó bride in a white dress with a lace kerchief and the dresser in a dark gown.

The works of the fifties are marked by realism, a concentration on the essential, deep psychological insight, the stylization and ornamentation variously emphasized. In general, the artist takes her themes from the lives of peasants, but in the years of the great transformation, in compliance with the thematic tendencies of the age, she occasionally represented industrial workers, for instance in *Glass-blower* and *Smelter* (1953); she also produced numerous scenes of the new way of life such as for instance *Folk Dance Group Rehearsing* (1952) or the *Relief with Dove of Peace*, made to celebrate the Liberation (1951).

For Margit Kovács the prime source of inspiration was the Hungarian village, the way of life, past and present, of the Hungarian people; to quote her own words: "I endeavour to seize in peasant figures the rich emotional diversity of life. I only visit peasants yet they provide me with most of my themes... It has been in young peasant girls and old peasant women that I have encountered in the purest form the feelings which are close to me and encourage me in my work."[69] This inspiration, her own tendency to lyricism, her keen powers of observation, the experience naturally acquired by a woman of a cheerful contemplative disposition throughout a life spent in a variety of circumstances, her substantial training as an artist and her aspirations towards clarity of form and harmony—all combined to permit the creation of a unique world of individual forms and ornamentation. The spell of every new invention enthralled her only briefly, her imagination being ever stirred by something new, so that she was able to fuse new life into past achievements and plastic ideas, and find relaxation in abundant ornamentation. Her techniques developed not so much chronologically but rather parallel to each other. She believed that there is no boundary separating her sculptural and ceramist veins or no more than the distinction that "... the ceramist starts in some measure from the potter and thence proceeds to sculpture", as in her figures turned on the wheel, which hardly ever deny in character their start "from the pot". In her own works Margit Kovács was unable to separate the sculptor from the ceramist. "Separation is out of the question, the two converge for the most part naturally. While turning the wheel I feel that there is no distinct boundary separating the work of the sculptor and the ceramist; they say the same thing in different dialects. Perhaps it may be said that this craft of handling clay—for me the most rapturous activity—offers innumerable possibilities. When one gets tired of pursuing one it is easy to change to another. When I have been modelling, it is a pleasure to turn to designing, engraving, making for instance a one-plane clay table—a very different proposition from kneading clay. To put it more accurately, I prepare strips —'gnocchi' as I call them—which I put together, constructing forms, figures. Thus at the very outset of the work there is a certain difference. A ceramist builds forms as does the swallow its nest. The sculptor, on the other hand, immediately puts compact forms on a framework of alien material, iron or wood. When I am working and feel inclined to stop for a breather but have no patience to stop, I find rest by simply changing my technique."[70]

It follows from the primarily self-expressing, lyrical character of her passion for creative work that she availed herself of the most varied possibilities of visual modes, her preference depending on their suitability for conveying a mood or emotion.

It is because of their sincerity that we find her works irresistible. This frankness is a fundamental trait of the artist's personality. As she herself said: "I trust my sincerity. I strive to express what is beautiful or the response I feel. I always want to be candid in my work. I live between two contrary poles. One is fear of extinction: I want to keep pace with the age. The other is fear lest I should let myself be driven into an insincere trend: lest I should fall behind time and life. But what is new in life I wish to assimilate and formulate in my own idiom. My idiom is identical with my personality."[71]

The times demanded a qualitative change in the way of life and to express this "new" life she had to represent in her works not delicate and refined ladies but earnest and sturdy Hungarian peasants. This approach to reality as well as an increasing emphasis on characterization are indicated as early as in the figures of the *Family Photograph Album* and can be quite clearly traced in painted murals, in the *Girl with Lily and Lamb*, a terracotta relief made about 1948 and in *Homewards* (1952), a work conceived in a mood of melancholy.

"New" features appear first in garments and the impedimenta appropriate to the figures, although the "folk costumes" in which Margit Kovács dressed her figures have never been worn anywhere; they are garments which she transformed and enriched to suit her own idea of what is decorative.

The murals painted around 1950 are conversation pieces in character. In its mood and in its impact, the *Turning the Wheel* (c. 1951) still stands quite near to the mural *Sleeping Beauty*. The boy facing to the right, moulding a narrow-necked jug on the wheel, is her own symbol; as in the *Boy at the Potter's Wheel* (1929), there are vases and pitchers on the shelves. In contrast to the almost monumental *Boy at the Potter's Wheel*, this work is more relaxed in composition, full of detail, richly coloured, and homely in atmosphere.

In *Meal in the Meadow* (1951), a harvester and his wife are represented having their midday meal on the stubble of a field. The woman in the left corner with her skirt tucked up is shown cutting bread, a theme that is often found in Margit Kovács's art of this period. In this picture the representation of the figures is realistic, though the background is indicated schematically by a few ears of wheat bending in the breeze and flowers opening here and there on the ground. The faces are delicate, the bare feet large and grotesque by comparison.

As the years passed she used more and more vivid colours. "Her fresh delicate colours and the flowing lines of some of her figures seem to reflect the most dynamic aspect of our own lives." However, critics did not altogether care for the stylized character of her figures; "There is a tendency to make her favourite figures of young girls too refined and ethereal. Her folk dancers are apt to recall Botticelli's 'Primavera', her peasant girls seem more like ladies of the court... In the case of murals one must doubt whether it is at all appropriate to use the technique which gives the colouring of the face and body a dull tone. This has the effect of making the most important parts of the representation—the faces—seem lifeless and dull when seen against the brilliant colours of the background."[72] At the same time *Folk Dance Group Rehearsing* and *Egg-painter*, a niche-relief, both dating from the same period, were recognized as works of outstanding value.

In the early fifties a change became noticeable in the design of her figures too; especially in the painted murals the figures became gentle, very sensitive, almost arabesque—traits which were further emphasized by too vivid colouring and an opulent use of popular ornamentation.

Of the murals produced in 1952, that painted on black tile, the *Apple Picking*, is one of her major works. Here, as in other one-plane compositions, perspective is solved by placing one scene above the other. The apple-tree, placed in the centre, dominates the composition with its profusely spreading leafy branches, a design reminiscent of those seen on Early Flemish carpets. On the right, a boy stands among the flowers under the tree, holding a ladder against the trunk; on the extreme right a peasant girl with braided hair and lace-trimmed petticoat holds up her apron, while the little boy sitting high in the branches gathers the apples. Beneath the tree the picture is enriched by a detail with something of the character of a still-life—a representation of a wheel-barrow and a wicker-basket full of apples. The modelling of the figures and the representation of the clothing are completely realistic, an effect accentuated by the use of white tints and varnish.

The monumental *Stove with Wedding Scenes*, in Vastagh House at Szentendre, is one of the principal exhibits of the Margit Kovács collection. In form it follows the lines of Renaissance stoves. The lattice-work mantel has a pattern representing birds pecking at grapes. The body of the stove is covered with large white glazed tiles profusely decorated with coloured motifs highlighted by varnish.

It was a momentous occasion in the history of Hungarian ceramics when the exhibition of the collected works of Margit Kovács opened in the Nemzeti Szalon in 1953. One hundred and sixty-five pieces were exhibited, from conic figurines measuring only fifteen or twenty centimetres to stoves two metres high. She had found the individual forms through which she could express herself as an artist; the turbulent period of seeking had given way to a period of serenity and assurance. She had reached the happy stage when theme, material and style presented themselves together and she had the talent to make use of them. Intuition, imagination, technique, personal experience, study and observation combined to give to her work a unique and individual glow of perfection.

Fame followed recognition and she was fêted at home and abroad. In 1953 she was awarded the distinction of Artist of Merit of the Hungarian People's Republic. In 1958 her work gained the Grand Prize of the World Exhibition in Brussels, and in 1959 she was selected as Honoured Artist of the Hungarian People's Republic. There was also an exhibition of her collected works in Rome. Wherever she exhibited —at the International Exhibition of Ceramics in Ostende in 1959 and in Prague in 1962—her work was always highly praised.

Of her most original works, the tales retold in the form of ceramics, she said: "The ceramist sees the world from a bird's-eye view, and this invariably lends a quality of unreality to the representation, as in a fairy tale. That is the association that comes to my mind: the bird's-eye view of reality and the tale. Things are seen differently according to whether one is a painter, a sculptor or a ceramist—the ceramist also looks for the tale in reality."[73]

Her remark concerning the ceramist's task of representing reality is an indication of her individual conception and creative methods: the ceramist "... does not reject the delights of weaving tales and of dreaming dreams; on the contrary these heighten her sense of reality; their magic enhances beauty, intensifies ugliness and clarifies reality by the sharpness of the delineation"[74].

Her individual world has taken shape. Her figures have a life of their own: they are happy, sad, meaningful. Her jugs and dishes "...glow in the light of magic; it is as if her pieces were unglazed, all their shimmering light aglow from within... from the creative force"[75], which is really the warm human touch of the creative artist. In these years Margit Kovács never paused in her creative activity, producing more and more of her artistic offspring: painted and modelled murals, jugs, figures, dishes, compositions enshrining scenes of folk life—sometimes without avoiding the danger of too prolific decoration to the detriment of composition, but this was always a passing phase.

Her high relief murals are masterpieces not only of her own lifework but also of all the fine arts in Hungary today. The Hungarian countryside also provided the artist with some of her themes. Wherever the composition includes a number of figures they are always closely grouped, an arrangement less frequently found in painted pictures. They are linked by the rhythm of the work, which is determined by the gestures and attitudes of the figures. The narrative quality is encouraged by the warm, emotional approach which, together with the ingenious and imaginative ornamentation, bestow on Margit Kovács's works an exquisite sense of completeness.

Her work is based on strict principles of composition as well as her knowledge of sculpture.

It is the grotesque features which most of all illustrate the liberating force of irony in works of this period. In this way her tendency to sentimentality is counterbalanced; she was able to develop her gift for evolving types, broadening the epic flow of her art while contriving to preserve the doctrinaire formulas of socialist realism.

In *Wedding* (1955)—one of her best works and a notable achievement in the history of ceramic art in Hungary—her figures are no longer types personifying a particular mood or attitude to life, they are individuals. Here her ironic disposition prevails, sharpening her representation of the emotional group of guests staring delightedly at the wedded couple.

The *Wine Harvest* (1955), executed in a variety of techniques, is another important work. Here again she enshrines a happy moment of life in the country. It is a highly imaginative work with a strongly narrative quality and the dreamlike atmosphere of an old fable.

When she was at the height of her powers figures modelled in the round assumed a more significant role. Genre pieces moulded on the wheel have brought beauty to hundreds of homes. It was in this period that she produced on the wheel large glazed figures, *Cutting the Loaf* (1952), *It Looks Like Rain* (1953) and, supreme among her major glazed pieces in realistic vein, *The Spinning Room* (1953). These figures demonstrate her virtuose technical ability. She exploited to the full all the possibilities of the potter's wheel: using a style suited to the material she introduced into her most realistic representations ironic, grotesque and decorative elements, thus producing monumental, modern pieces of improving techniques once used to create the finest examples of folk art. In making these figures she had to solve the artistic and technical problems of increasing motion and mobilization of the forms and surfaces of large, turned areas. The simplest and most harmonious solution is exemplified in the calm standing figure with raised head, clad in bodice and long skirt, *It Looks Like Rain*. In *Cutting the Loaf* a stimulating composition is created by connecting closed spherical and cylindrical forms. These form problems began to absorb her attention from the late fifties. Ornamentation is also assigned a more outstanding role on the garments of women dressed in folk costume.

In these large, turned figures characterization and ornamentation combine to meet the loftiest requirements of sculpture within the possibilities of ceramic art.

This was the period when she produced a succession of gorgeous dishes, jugs, birds, animal-shaped vessels. Technical virtuosity in engraving, painting and mixing the glazes, a zest for flowing narrative, a unique way of making use of popular ornamental motifs give her work an unmistakable identity.

After 1956 the official attitude to art began to change and a new generation of ceramists influenced by the work of István

Gádor began to find recognition; indeed their fresh conception and new aesthetic views exerted an influence on members of the older generation. Today the majority of Hungarian ceramists are associated with one or two quite opposing trends. One group is faithful to Hungarian traditions and the spirit of folk art; though influenced by contemporary artistic trends they nevertheless retain their own peculiar form idiom and make use of certain characteristic features of the forms and ornamentation of folk pottery. The other trend is towards monumental ceramics in the new constructivist style found in Western Europe. Among the first group there are artists who, influenced by West European ceramics, became followers of a Japanese trend related to Zen-Buddhism. They produce pieces which resemble the spontaneous phenomena found in nature, e.g. water-washed, moss-covered stone, or recreate the simplified organic shapes of nature. Among these artists are several older ceramists, for instance Imre Schrammel, Lívia Gorka. This trend is a late product of romanticism, a reaction to the overwhelming civilization of consumer society.

In 1956 Margit Kovács sensed the arrival of a new taste in ceramics. Her murals the *Belle of the Village* and *Medieval Grape Harvest* (1956) are unchanged in design and convey the same message as previous works but the composition no longer includes so many figures in movement and the colour schemes are also more subdued.

The *Swineherd* (1956), seen blowing his horn, is engraved with new, simpler patterns and it is concentrated in one block, calling to mind the forms and technique found in popular wood carving.

After 1956 the traditions and ornamental motifs of folk art lost some of their attraction for Hungarian ceramists. Decoration was more sparse, and with the new wave of Bauhaus there arrived a geometrical, constructivist trend and a search for archaic, simplified, tectonic forms.

The potter's wheel was less frequently used; vessels and figures were built up from strips of clay, forms were asymmetrical like pieces of natural rock or shingle; large vases reminiscent of ancient forms were produced with rough surfaces, glazed and unglazed, to give unusual and remarkable effects.

Since World War II terracotta has been consistently superseded in European ceramics by fire-clay with a rough surface fired at high temperatures, a material which calls for different elaboration of forms and glazes, unlike the handling of highly flexible clay.

As a student at Sèvres Margit Kovács had learnt how to treat fire-clay; her *Plump-cheeked Girl* with a surface which is still modern and exciting in its effect, created a sensation in its own time because of its archaic forms.

After 1956, modern, revolutionary artistic tendencies, attempting to express reality and favouring abstraction, indirectly helped Margit Kovács to experience a new creative period. Her development since 1956 and her great achievements of the past decade reveal a succession of different, often conflicting, influences.

Commenting on the experiments she made at the peak of her career and the courage necessary for seeking new methods she declared: "I think it natural. One always harbours the latent fear of coming to a halt, of being swept into a groove, of falling victim to routine. Art is a ceaseless search, and, I believe, even more so in this revolutionary, restlessly seeking age. The artist is in permanent quest, trying to build up his own art, to find what is new, and from what is new that which he desires most to call his own. And one tries to avoid what is only a fashion."[76]

The material to be used compelled her to evolve a new form idiom. "A couple of years ago I was given for a certain work a coarser, fire-clay-like material. Its colour was pure joy, and it was a delight to press it in your hands. It was happiness to work with it. The coarseness of the material compelled me to devise a more rustic form, corresponding to the task, to dismiss details and to model more strictly than hitherto. The material enjoined strictness."[77]

About 1956 she resumed the use of fire-clay. She took a fancy to it, and she has herself confessed: "The possibilities inherent in clay tempt one to model too smoothly. Therefore I like to add now and then fire-clay of coarser nature to my clay, letting the material practically force me to model larger, more comprehensive forms."[78]

Her first exquisite pieces in fire-clay were figurines: *The Kiss of Judas* (1956), *Fisherman* (1958), *Sleeping Boy* (1958), *Old Fisherman* (1958), and *Old Shepherd* (1958).

With these more vigorous, more rugged, more comprehensive forms Margit Kovács returned to the human proportions and archaic flavour of her early works. Once again her figures became dumpy, with large heads and hands and uncouth legs, like the relief figures seen in Romanesque cathedrals; also in moulding she reverted to an expressive treatment, to apparently perfunctorily executed, unfinished surfaces.

As always in periods of transition it was some time before the new forms she created could be seen to dominate her work.

Even the coloured and glazed terracotta, a narrative mural painted in 1961 entitled *In Remembrance of Things Past*, is a scene of tapestry-like effect, though it is inspired not by folk tales bu tby Late Gothic miniatures. The design is simple, the figures are harmoniously moulded. The atmosphere is tranquil giving no sign of ecstasy and there are no jostling crowds. The picture is suffused with a certain exalted seriousness.

New forms, thoughts and moods touched by sadness produced some splendid works that will certainly endure, for instance the large reliefs from the late fifties, *"Hey, Fishermen, Fishermen"* (1958), an expressive ruggedly moulded work in the spirit of Hungarian folk song, and *Sleeping Mother Earth and the Four Seasons* (1959). Their effect is archaic, sincere: an enduring human concept infused into forms of arresting simplicity. *Sleeping Mother Earth and the Four Seasons* was modelled for the World Meteorological Organization in Geneva. Reticence and simplicity are emphasized by forgoing the use of colours. Fire-clay reliefs and figures from the late fifties retain the original colour of the material. A liking for subdued harmonies is seen in works from the end of her first period and again in the fifties after a period when she used vivid colours. In these years she discovered the beauty of simplicity and was attracted by the delicacy of hues which are evoked in fire-clay by light and shade. Her figures are concentrated, self-contained. The message is conveyed by their attitudes and by their direct, revealing gestures.

In the terracotta relief *OMI 1860–1960* commissioned in 1960 by the National Meteorological Institute to celebrate the 100th anniversary of its foundation, Margit Kovács developed still further her technique of fire-clay modelling. The composition is divided into irregular sections, the figure of the meteorologist, moulded like a medieval monk, being placed in the centre. The other figures, personifying elements of nature, are grouped about the principal figure as in early engraved maps. Two figures of running angels, one on either side, are depicted bearing lightning to symbolize storm; the upright female figure with a shawl on her head signifies fog, the boy blowing a horn in the left upper corner represents the wind; and the boy in the right upper corner pouring water from a jug, rain. The disc of the sun appears in the central upper section. The inscription consists of characters looped to one another. Here Margit Kovács's zest for ornamentation, so evident in her early products, again comes into its own, and was to be allowed even wider scope in later works (*Affinity*, 1970).

In the lower section of the relief three allegorical couples symbolize the eternal cycle of nature.

In the terracotta mural modelled in 1961, "*Two Girls Went to Pick Flowers*", the artist reverted to more decorative solutions. Backgrounds are again adorned with protuberant flowers, the petals being decorated with men's names written with curvilinear flourishes. The meandering lines of minor pieces moulded in the round also recall her early works but here she incorporates new methods, and she also experiments in a variety of ways.

The Kiss of Judas, modelled about the year 1956, is the product of a lifetime's experience: the peasant face of Jesus expresses everything that a man may feel in the face of certain death.

The *Old Fisherman* (1958), dragging a heavily laden net to the shore, represents the willows by the river Tisza, yet reminds one inevitably of Hemingway's "The Old Man and the Sea". The experience of growing old, the awareness of "time's winged chariot", engaged the attention of Margit Kovács ever more frequently from the year 1956. When she was painting the mural *Norn* in the years 1947–48 the thought of death had been present in her mind, but in the fever of free and full creative activity, success and world fame she had not fully realized its tragic implications.

She was still engrossed in an attempt to devise new techniques by which she could make use of the potter's wheel. She incorporated the increasingly complex potter's shapes into her individual artistic world, in which form became the visible expression of accumulated humanist content. Form and content are difficult to separate in her works. To quote her own words: "In most instances the two are so closely entangled that it is downright impossible to separate them. Sometimes the first impulse to do a work is precipitated by some emotion or thought. But it has also happened that the idea came from a lump of clay in my hand. A small cake of clay is enough to produce a sketch by kneading and shaping."[79]

The question of modernity and tradition also occupied her mind. Forms that were closed but in every dimension mobile, dynamic and rhythmic, were again imbued with the traditional shapes and ornamental motifs of folk art. *Madonna with Babe-in-arms* (c. 1959) and *Mother with Child* (c. 1960) were late successors of *Nursing Mother* and *The Spinning Room*, further links in the chain of her artistic development.

Simultaneously with the appearance of unglazed, uncoloured fire-clay figures where the form is simple and the surfaces rough, she was making another group of figures, also turned on the wheel, but this time aiming at completely closed forms, a more geometric construction, a motionless, timeless monumentality, in complete contrast to mobilized globular forms. The theme here is weeping for the dead, mourning, suffering. Here we find drama in clay. Her *Mourner* (1958), wearing a big shawl and full skirts, is compressed into a truncated cone form, staring ahead with an empty look in her eyes, her large sinewy hands on her knees. Margit Kovács uses the conventional posture for the expression of pain but the figure is the very personification of mourning.

The upright figure of *Mourning I* modelled in 1960 is more passionate, expressing the pain of shock. This figure, too, is a masterpiece of the "stern" style. The figure, compressed in cylindrical form, is depicted closely wrapped in a shawl which almost covers the head in the traditional country style. As in her figures of professional mourners (1951), the folds of the garments are indicated only by etching; only above the feet is there one section of moulded drapery. The features, engraved and only partially visible through the fingers of two hands, are ravaged with pain.

Around the year 1960 round and hemispherical jug-like forms, natural products of the wheel, were used for the creation of softly billowing, closed figures of classical beauty. Margit Kovács was deeply absorbed in the problems of technique and composition posed by the creation of groups of several figures from a single vessel.

Two of her finest pieces turned on the wheel, in the form

of gently undulating vessels, depict the meeting of Mary and Elizabeth, a group of mugs of which there are two examples, the *Visitation* and *How Nice to See You Again* (both from 1958) and the *Daydreamer* (1960–62).

In the large, elaborate figure of *Madonna with Babe-in-arms*, modelled in the same period, the artist reverted to the treatment of form seen in *The Spinning Room*. In construction and composition the small *Peasant Madonna* is the most dynamic of all her major figures turned on the wheel; here turning and free modelling were combined. The contours are also more mobile than in any preceding plastic composition.

The chamotte-clay frieze in relief, *Man and Work*, was originally modelled in 1961 for the façade of the Cultural Centre of the Csepel Motor Factory. On this frieze, eight metres in length, there are representations of Adam and Eve in Paradise; there is also a new variant of the *Potter* and other crafts are represented by a bricklayer building a wall, a carpenter, a miller and a goldsmith. But there are also references to the arts: suspended masks symbolize the theatre, one figure is shown reciting poetry and a musician plays his lute. The work was very popular when shown at the Exhibition of Hungarian Applied Arts in Turin. The Hungarian State presented the work to the City of Turin where it may be seen in the Galleria dell'Arte Moderna.

In the years 1961–62 the art of Margit Kovács moved into a new dimension. In the high relief in terracotta, the *Market* (1961), she developed themes and ideas used in the friezes made for the Csepel Motor Factory. But in this small work Margit Kovács made use of childhood memories. A market-woman is seen weighing apples while a fishwife sits in a tent with a pannier of fish for sale. These are genre scenes with a rustic atmosphere of warmth and gaiety now rarely experienced in the impersonal atmosphere of city supermarkets. It expresses our nostalgia and longing for the relief of warm, direct human contacts.

The world of Margit Kovács evokes a way of life which has passed away, the essentially archaic and conservative world of peasant life in the villages. Her form idiom is rooted in this world, particularly that of the fire-clay figures. Thus Margit Kovács followed the trend which among exponents of the fine arts would now be categorized as 'archaic'.

Old Fisherman and *Sleeping Boy* were followed by works in similar vein, for instance *Woman Carrying a Bundle of Twigs*, a figure bowed under the weight of her bundle (*c.* 1962) and *Market-woman*, a seated figure clad in full skirts, waiting to sell her chickens (*c.* 1962). Here the style, like that of figures turned on the wheel, is marked by more closed forms and a less expansive spirit.

The Retrospective Exhibition of Margit Kovács held in 1962 was so successful that is was prolonged for two weeks. At last her work was accepted by critics who had previously persisted in raising the question of whether or not her works were behind the times.

The art of Margit Kovács had been tempered, her world was accepted, almost classical; it was a unique world, imbued with something from every new trend she personally had found congenial. The process of assimilation had been gradual, but from her hands came masterpieces which could only have come into existence at that moment in time.

Although her exhibition attracted thousands of visitors and her work became more and more famous both at home and abroad, no commission came her way, as stated in 1962.[80]

When interviewed in 1966 she said, "At present I have no commissions. I do not complain; sometimes it is good to have a period without engagements when one can let one's imagination roam and feel completely free to do what one chooses—murals, figures or vessels. In such a period one relaxes and at the same time prepares oneself for new ventures; finally one reaches the point where there is no danger of repeating oneself in the next work."[81]

She was able to live on the income of her serialized ceramics; nevertheless she worked with untiring zeal. She enlarged her forms, mingled techniques. Her figures became ever more monumental. It was the period when her imagination was fired by the art of ancient cultures; for instance, the inspiration for *Centaur* (1966–67) would seem to have been early Greek art.

She did get commissions now and then. *In the Woods*, a narrative mural (1965) for a wall in the Home for Crippled Children in Budapest, reveals a variety of techniques; she used tiles in a variety of sizes to create an elaborate carpet-like design with representations of stags, deer, foxes, hares, lions and a boy beneath a tree blowing his pipe. It was at this time that she modelled her high relief *Pagan Grove* depicting a faun and a nymph dancing in the forest and a centaur blowing a horn. In elaborating the braided design of the branches of trees in the background she gave free rein to her love of decorative detail.

In a fire-clay relief composed of irregular segments, *Dreaming–The Shepherd and His Flock* (1965), she invoked the timeless world of mythology and folk tales.

The small chamotte clay figures, about 50 cm in height, made during the last decade, form a new synthesis in her art. In these works she gave expression to her individual view of life in figures in which the modelling is confined to the essential, the form expressive; figures are imbued with her own sense of humour, self-deprecating irony and elegiac reflections.

These chamotte clay figures expressing the unique world in which she moved are rainbow-coloured. Three of these works date from 1966: *Nursing the Sick I, Fatigue*—the seated figure of a woman with her hands resting in her lap—and *Winding the Yarn; David*—depicted with his lyre—dates from 1967, the *Chestnut-roaster*, which was exhibited at the First National Biennale of Ceramics in Pécs, and *Vigil* date from 1968. All these, together with *Birth*, a group composition, *Marriage* (1968) modelled after her experiments in turning forms in pairs, *Death* (1968), a terse, dramatic composition of five figures, the *Anglers* (1968) and *Mother and Daughter* (1968), daughter kneeling enfolded in her mother's comforting arms—all are outstanding examples of her work and express the widest possible range of human emotions.

In some of her narrative works based on traditional tales she incorporates incidents described in the Bible, as for instance in *Angel Watching for a Secret* (1967) and *Expulsion from Paradise* (1967).

The tense rhythm of the geometrical figures in *Mourners* is repeated in an even more masterly composition, *Fishermen's Wives* (1968); here the five figures seem to have been frozen into immobility by their long watch for the return of their loved ones.

In the latest pieces monumentality comes from content—the message for humanity expressed in the moulding of the figures.

In *Old People Feasting in Silence* (1969–70), a relief in white earth colours, the atmosphere is reminiscent of a medieval miniature and expresses the sadness of old age and the approach of death. The modelling reveals the love and compassion with which she represented a variety of temperaments. It was her aim to express in her own idiom the ways in which individual human beings face the approach of old age. This concentration of content necessitated new modes of expression for which she had to work out a new type of structure.

In the late sixties her figures of terracotta and fire-glaze became geometrically simplified, taking on cylindrical shapes.

In *Annunciation III* (1968), the figures are imbued with the naive piety of the carved saints seen in Gothic cathedrals, and here again the artist had to contend with the limited possibilities afforded by the potter's wheel for the production of a work over 80 cm. high. A series of figures were produced in this terse idiom of turned tubular forms simplified to essentials and elongated to a height of around one metre—*The World Is Beautiful* (1968), *The Bugler* (1968–70), *Theatre* (1969), *Shepherds* (1968) and *Philemon and Baucis* (1970).

In the work of Margit Kovács there is a masterly and profound fusion of form, plasticity, colour, and ornamentation; the decorative element therefore has a place in her art which is just as significant as sculptural development of forms. The new plastic synthesis she has worked out lies within the framework of her own decorative world; when held in check in the first stage of creative activity, as in the case of small fire-clay figures, this ornamental vein asserts itself irresistibly in the second stage. Moreover, when it has been for too long suppressed, it overrides the forms and weakens the composition. Such times are low-water marks of the creative period.

It was one of the events of the year when her new works were exhibited in 1970 in the Art Gallery, Budapest. Most of the works shown had been produced between 1960–70. The critics gave high praise: "... visitors were delighted by the astonishing richness of this harvest; splendour of colour, variety of idiom, delicacy of touch, one figure displaying details fine as lace, another full of dramatic intensity; ideas expressed with terse simplicity, the essence only; nostalgic memories of Hungarian peasant carvings are revived in figures with trumpets, others have the unself-conscious rigidity of Byzantine representations of saints; we find echoes of the mysticism expressed in eastern cupolas, the wry and meek godliness found in the carvings of saints on the columns of medieval cathedrals. As many forms of giving expression to feelings as there are works, a plentiful flow of creative abundance."[82] "Life moulded in clay."[83] "We are witnessing magic"[84] "...of course, the artist herself remains a fairy-being for ever to all her friends and all who have come under her spell, but her art has outgrown fairyland... Like nature, her works present us with the fullness of human existence in all its details... Her art is like a phenomenon of nature. The material and intellectual fusion of her talent is like a solitary tree teeming with life, growing richer from year to year and renewing itself while growing incessantly, shooting ever more new branches, opening ever more beautiful, more fragrant flowers, bearing ever more desirable, ever more delicious fruit—yet, in essence, the tree remains the same that once sprouted from the seed of original genius."[85]

"Every aspect of the artist's work now on view can be traced back to her earliest efforts: in them we can see already the conception, the orientation, even the idioms and techniques of these mature products of her art. Over the years she has become mistress of the materials and instruments of her craft. With her hands she has given to her figures material existence, but she has also imbued them with the very breath of human life."[86]

In the sixties Margit Kovács fell under the spell of Szentendre where there is now a permanent exhibition of her work in Vastagh House. Her source of inspiration was no longer the melancholy saints and provincial Christs seen on icons but simple human beings enduring the tribulations of earthly existence.

The influence of Szentendre transformed her approach profoundly. She began to produce works which summarize all her achievements. She began to incorporate all the stylistic features of her early work but in a purified form, while both modelling and techniques are of a higher order. In her figures made of fire-clay the expressionism of earlier forms gave way before dramatic effects that are almost crude, and on the few human-shaped vessels the decorative impulse inspired by Jaschik has a grotesque quality (*Sirens*, 1968–69; *Odysseus*, 1967). Elsewhere ornamental open-work was refined and more lace-like (*Royal Betrothal*, 1970; *The Dance of Salome*, 1969; *The Good and the Wicked Fairy*, 1970). The terseness of forms reached an extremity in geometrically simplified, column-like figures with an upward sweeping movement: (*The Bugler*, 1968–70; *Mean Old Women*, 1967; *Annunciation III*, 1968; *Funeral Oration*, 1970.)

In contrast to the Gothic elongation of her large and increasingly incorporeal turned forms—which was the idiom in which Margit Kovács finally abstracted her lyricism—we find in the plastic execution of her small fire-clay figures and mural works the thick-set, compressed forms of the Middle Ages. This is a highly characteristic interpretation which has been described by Máté Major, "What is naive is a shade more naive, what is grotesque is yet more grotesque, what is angular is still more angular, what is round is more round. She adds a difference here and there, just enough to bring her work into our own age, while conforming to the mainstream of developments in art; her own art bears the mark of a single-minded artist who is both intuitive and individual."[87]

Transposing her own experiences, she stylized the essential into plane-like ornamentation, as in *Nocturnal Magic of the Forest* (1969) and the bas-relief *Cantata Profana* inspired by the music of Bartók (1969–70); in the former by rhythmic representation of trees and animals with human faces, in the latter by an abstract conception of the figures of stags.

In her later work the figures were constructed in cylindrical, conic and globular geometrical forms, for instance *The Patroness of Onion-Domes* inspired by the Serbian churches of Szentendre (1968), the brilliantly executed *Hommage à Szentendre* (1968), *"Oh, Venice!"*, and *Seated Madonna* modelled in 1972, in which she reverted to the Byzantine effects found in her early works.

The stylized *Seated Madonna*, a crowned figure on a chair, was modelled in 1972 and intended for Buda Castle. The theme was modelled in two forms: one elongated in the Gothic style of her latest figures *(Gothic Madonna)*, the other in the spirit of the Serbian icons of Szentendre. When the statues were unveiled, Margit Kovács declared, "Around the slender figure one is aware of the surrounding space; but the little plump figure has made the place so intimately her own that it seems she has always been there".

From the year 1967 her figures had been growing longer, the heads small and increasingly generalized as types, each one representing a particular psychological make-up. The features are indicated by a few engraved lines by which she expresses a whole outlook on life, a human destiny. The change in the mental outlook of these figures illustrates her departure from the artistic innovations of the fifties. Her figures are mostly meditative, sad, lonely; even joyous moments are increasingly touched with sadness (*Beggar-woman with Forget-me-not Blue Eyes*, 1970, and *Sunday*, 1973).

Her gift for delineating character and human nature became more profound with the passage of the years.

In her figures in the Gothic style motion is minimal, the silhouette self-contained, while the frontal aspect reminds us of Egyptian statues. The bodies are merely outlined, with only hands and heads. Colour is less frequently employed, often totally absent, though sometimes soft pastel hues are used to concentrate the increasingly blocklike forms of the figures. Little glaze is used only where it plays a role in ornamentation, for instance on the hem of garments or on crowns. The colours she most favoured were yellow und turquoise. In the execution of faces and eyes she resumed her old technique of painting the pupils and the mouth.

In certain major works this artistic method is strangely powerful, as in *Funeral Oration* (1970), in which she conveyed a painful recognition of the inevitability of death by her rigid representation of a timeless moment.

Her latest work is a monumental frieze consisting of a series of ten high reliefs representing the history of Győr; here Margit Kovács revived the forms of her first expressive period by seeking and finding new associations. It is a brilliantly conceived composition depicting the principal events in the history of this ancient town. The reliefs were created for close inspection, the forms reminiscent of those stemming from the reliefs of Early Romanesque cathedrals.

The art of Margit Kovács showed a remarkable capacity for assimilation. She drew on medieval Christian and Byzantine art as well as on the endeavours of her contemporaries. She emphatically accepted tradition, and used her own early methods with a new content. Her new series of reliefs was based on the dynamic antithesis of old and new solutions of form. She represented moments of struggle, work, mourning and happiness, for her experience of life has always been rooted in emotional rather than intellectual relationships.

In her latest works she also achieved synthesis in her decorative solutions; in the railing of fourfold rows of square holes which separates the individual reliefs in the frieze at Győr the geometric style harmonizes perfectly with the open-work ornamentation of the flower-pot rests and lamp frames already in position.

The platters, jugs, vases and cylindrical animal figures created by Margit Kovács are primarily intended to give pleasure in the home, their practical functional use being of only secondary consideration.

Since the exhibition in the Tamás Gallery her vessels have been characterized by richer colours and more elaborate forms—which, however, always retain a highly individual flavour; also by a strong tendency to ornamentation. These features have become more marked with the passage of time.

Compositions, turned on the wheel, in which the form combines human and animal figures, are particularly characteristic of her work, a bold connection which not infrequently produces a bizarre effect (*On Camelback*, 1959). One early, still functional representative of this trend is the splendid jug *"Fluctuat nec mergitur"* (1948–49), which symbolizes a barque tossed by waves; on the prow is the turned figure of a mermaid, her eyes searching the horizon.

Animal subjects constitute the majority of her figures turned on the wheel. The series of animal figures dating from the fifties, *Bull*, *Duck* and *Pigeon*, was developed further in her *Dragon*; and the figure of a lion is found again and again during the course of her career. The prototype of *Snarling Lion* (1957) can also be found among her first pieces turned on the wheel, but the small *Lion* (1950) was based on a quite new conception of the subject.

In the hollow centre of her dishes she began to model high reliefs, creating new works related in technique to niche-reliefs and representing a further development in the plastic arts. The rims are broad and flat, emphasizing the highly decorative character of the inscriptions which are sometimes painted, sometimes plastic.

The dish commemorating the fortieth anniversary of the wedding day of Gyula Kaesz and his wife, Kató Lukáts, is one of her finest achievements. She was closely linked for decades both as artist and friend to the couple; Gyula Kaesz had been one of those responsible for raising the standard of applied arts in Hungary to a European level, and Kató Lukáts was a gifted illustrator and graphic artist. Her hands were guided by remembrance and love when she moulded in a shallow bowl the figures of Adam and Eve, the ancient symbols of marriage. The smooth wide rim is separated from the bowl of the dish by a laurel wreath in relief. The composition is circular, with strong effects of light and shade; it would seem that the inspiration was not unconnected with the tender, lyrical representations of her first period and also *Paradise* (1929). Here, too, the apple-tree of the Garden of Eden occupies the centre of the relief, while the serpent coiling itself round the trunk symbolizes destiny. The figures of Adam and Eve, although they might be described as charmingly clumsy, are more fragile and more coarsely moulded than the figures in *Paradise*, which symbolizes the fleeting character of youth and love.

The Father, the Son and the Ass (1968–70), an ornamental dish illustrating a fable, resembles in both form and composition *Commemorative Dish to the 40th Wedding Anniversary of Gyula Kaesz and His Wife* differing only in that the inscription on the wide rim is not modelled but painted. Between the words of the inscription are the heads of women, their expression indicating their reactions to the characters in the fable. The scene itself, moulded in the bowl of the dish, is rather grotesque, with a strong tendency to caricature. In the design of the characters she availed herself of the "bending blades of grass" motif seen on *Dish with Lizard* (1949).

In the composition of three figures in the round entitled *Be Good!* (1968) the technique stems from that of Renaissance works; the composition has a rhythm by which a link is forged between the figure of the mother, seated, and her two children. However, in contrast to the calm structural conception of Renaissance works, here there is a feeling of movement created by the undulating lines connecting the forms. This undulating linear connection has been applied by Margit Kovács during various periods of her activity, as for example on the niche-relief of the stirring work *Noah and his Wife* made in 1968–70.

Be Good! and *Noah and His Wife*, the symbol of human endurance and allusions to our endangered era, evidence the belief, like most of Margit Kovács's works, that—as Gyula Illyés wrote—"The world is not lost; we must endure. Our souls have been crushed, our beliefs are in ruins, particularly the famous stone tablets lie in fragments; it is nevertheless worth believing in the reconstruction of the world... that we can conquer, always and forever, that inanimate matter, death... that the future belongs to us, to the human race." Margit Kovács expressed the national character of the Hungarian people and, with her understanding of humanism, interpreted the problems posed by their philosophy of life, at the same time creating works of art comparable to any in the world.

*

On June 4th, 1977, after the first publication of this book, Margit Kovács died at the age of 75. Her swan-song was the *Stations of the Cross* of the Catholic church of Hollóháza in which she paid her last tribute to life irretrievable. Because she was an artist, and because she was alone—very much alone towards the end—looking her approaching death in the eye, in the story of Christ's suffering, anguish and pain, and in its promise of better days to come, she gave form to her own fate.

She worked indefatigably till the end, for she was in love with her calling. As she stated a short time before her death, "Clay is my daily bread, my joy and my sorrow. At first touch, it became an organic part of my life. And ever since, this material, making its way through my bloodstream, whirls me to heights of delight and, at times, plunges me into the valley of despair."

Ilona Pataky-Brestyánszky

Budapest, April 1978

1 PÓK, L.: *A szecesszió* [The Art Nouveau]. Budapest, 1972, p. 65.

2 NÉMETH, L.: *A művészet sorsfordulója* [The Peripeteia of Art]. Budapest, 1970, p. 30.

3 VAS, I.: *Nehéz szerelem* [A Difficult Love]. Budapest, 1963, p. 15.

4 [PATAKY-] BRESTYÁNSZKY, I.: *Modern magyar kerámia* [Modern Hungarian Ceramics]. Budapest, 1965, p. 48.

5 PATAKY, D.-né [BRESTYÁNSZKY, I.]: *A Zsolnay kerámia* [Zsolnay Majolica]. Budapest, 1955, p. 8.

6 PATAKY, D.-né [BRESTYÁNSZKY, I.]: op. cit., p. 10.

7–18 [PATAKY-] BRESTYÁNSZKY, I.: *Modern magyar kerámia* [Modern Hungarian Ceramics]. Budapest, 1965, pp. 8–9.

19 RADNAI–SZÖRÉNYI, I.: "Sèvres-től és Koppenhágától a komáromi újtemplomig" [From Sèvres and Copenhagen to the New Church of Komárom]. *Új Magyarság*, July 26, 1936, p. 15.

20 B. I.: "Minél több embernek örömet szerezni" [To Give Pleasure to as Many People as Possible]. *Magyar Nemzet*, July 2, 1950.

21 F. J.: "Simon György kiállítása" [Exhibition of Works by György Simon]. *Pesti Hírlap*, December 3, 1929.

22 *398th Collective Show*. June 1928, Nemzeti Szalon.

23, 24 *Magyar Iparművészet*, 1929, p. 58.

25 ANDOCSY, G.: "A magyar iparművészet nehéz napjai" [Hard Times for the Applied Arts in Hungary]. *Magyar Iparművészet*, 1929, p. 185.

26 *Magyar Iparművészet*, 1929, p. 82.

27 KÖRNER, É.: *Derkovits*. Budapest, 1968, p. 18.

28 FARKAS, E.: "Új forma" [New Forms]. *Magyar Iparművészet*, 1929, p. 8.

29 *Magyar Iparművészet*, 1930, p. 135.

30 PÓK, L.: op. cit., p. 442.

31 *Magyar Iparművészet*, 1930, p. 121.

32 *Magyar Iparművészet*, 1930, pp. 74–76.

33 *Magyar Iparművészet*, 1931, pp. 7–8.

34 PÓK, L.: op. cit., p. 420.

35 PÓK, L.: op. cit., p. 478.

36 PÓK, L.: op. cit., p. 432.

37, 38 PÓK, L.: op. cit., p. 411.

39, 40 "Address by J. Varga, Minister of Industry, in 1942, at the opening of the First Hungarian Exhibition of Glazed Pottery." *Magyar Iparművészet*, 1943, p. 40.

41 From the photographic archives of Ferenc Haár. By the courtesy of Lajos Lengyel.

42 RUFFY, P.: "Egy magyar művész" [A Hungarian Artist]. *Asszonyok*, May 14, 1964, p. 12.

43 M. I.: "Kovács Margit keramikai kiállítása a Tamás Galériában" [Exhibition of Ceramics by Margit Kovács at the Tamás Gallery]. *Magyarország*, November 24, 1935.

44, 45 "Kovács Margit keramikus" [Margit Kovács, Ceramist]. *Magyar Iparművészet*, 1935, p. 251.

46, 47 From the photographic archives of Ferenc Haár.

48, 49 MIHALIK, S.: "Az iparművészet Magyarországon" [Applied Arts in Hungary]. *Magyar Iparművészet*, 1937, p. 224.

50 F. J.: Article in *Pesti Hírlap*, December 18, 1938.

51 "Három művész a Tamás Galériában" [Three Artists at the Tamás Gallery]. *Esti Kurír*, December 13, 1938.

52, 53 *Új Magyarság*, quotation form an article, July 26, 1936.

54 R. P.: "Az élő magyar kerámia seregszemléje" [Review of Contemporary Hungarian Ceramics]. *Magyarország*, December 6, 1942.

55 *Magyar Iparművészet*, 1942, p. 41.

56 *Új Magyarság*, March 31, 1942.

57, 58 MIHALIK, S.: "Kovács Margit". *Magyar Iparművészet*, 1943, p. 92.

59 "Egyházművészet a lakásban" [Sacred Art in the Home]. Budapest, 1944. Catalogue of Exhibition.

60 BOBROVSZKY, I.: *Kovács Margit*. Budapest, 1961, p. 19.

61 B. I.: "Minél több embernek örömet szerezni" [To Give Pleasure to as Many People as Possible]. *Magyar Nemzet*, July 2, 1950.

62 K. M.: "Minden erőmmel és képességemmel" [With all My Might and all My Gifts]. *Magyar Nép*, May 30, 1948.

63 DOMANOVSZKY, Gy.: "Kerámiánk mai helyzete. I. nemzedék" [Hungarian Ceramics Today: the First Generation]. *Művészet*, 1964.

64 GÁCH, M.: "Egy óra Kovács Margittal" [An Hour with Margit Kovács]. *Magyar Nemzet*, July 1953.

65 RÉNYI, P.: Article in the *Szabad Nép*. July 17, 1952, p. 7.

66 B. I.: "Minél több embernek örömet szerezni" [To Give Pleasure to as Many People as Possible]. *Magyar Nemzet*, July 2,1950.

67 ARADI, N.: *Daumier, Derkovits és utódaik* [Daumier, Derkovits and Their Successors]. Budapest, 1968, p. 319.

68 NOBEL, F.: "Kovács Margit új alkotása" [A New Work by Margit Kovács]. *Építés–Építészet* (1950), 5.

69 FRANK, J.: "Kovács Margitnál" [A Visit to Margit Kovács]. *Élet és Irodalom*, February 5, 1966.

70 BOJÁR, I.: "Szerelme a mesterség" [In Love with Her Craft]. *Magyar Hírlap*, November 30, 1972.

71 NÁDAS, P.: "Ön kivel készítene interjút? Kovács Margittal" [Whom Would You Like to Interview? Margit Kovács]. *Pest megyei Hírlap*, January 29, 1967.

72 RÉNYI, P.: op. cit.

73, 74 B. I.: "Minél több embernek örömet szerezni" [To Give Pleasure to as Many People as Possible]. *Magyar Nemzet*, July 2, 1950.

75 BOLDIZSÁR, I.: "A Tündér" [The Fairy]. *Tükör*, March 12, 1962.

76, 77 FÖLDES, A.: "Útmutatás a szigorúsághoz" [Guide to Severity]. *Nők Lapja*, November 1966.

78 BOJÁR, I.: op. cit.

79 FÖLDES, A.: op. cit.

80 KAESZ, Gy.: "Kovács Margit kerámiakiállítása az Ernst Múzeumban" [Exhibition of Ceramics by Margit Kovács at the Ernst Museum]. *Magyar Nemzet*, April 15, 1962.

81 FÖLDES, A.: op. cit.

82 [PATAKY-] BRESTYÁNSZKY, I.: "Kovács Margitról" [About Margit Kovács]. *Művészet*, November 1970.

83 HAMAR, I.: "Agyagba formált élet" [Life Moulded in Clay]. *Kisalföld*, March 20, 1971.

84 MEDVE, I.: "Varázslat tanúi vagyunk" [We Are Witnessing Magic]. *Kisalföld*, August 1, 1971.

85, 86 BOLDIZSÁR, I.: op. cit.

87 MAJOR, M.: "Kovács Margit keramikusművész kiállítása" [Exhibition of Works by the Ceramist Margit Kovács]. Catalogue, Preface. 1970, p. 2.

A szecesszió Magyarországon [Art Nouveau in Hungary. Catalogue of the Székesfehérvár exhibition]. Budapest, 1951.

BAHR, H.: *Secession*, Vienna, 1900.

BOBROVSZKY, I.: *Kovács Margit.* Képzőművészeti Alap Kiadóvállalata, Budapest, 1961.

COX, E.: *Pottery and Porcelain.* New York, 1959.

CRANE, W.: *Line and Form.* London, 1900.

CREMONA, I.: *Il tempo dell'Art Nouveau.* Florence, 1904.

CSÁNYI, K.: *A magyar kerámia és porcelán története és jegyei* [The History and Characteristics of Hungarian Ceramics and Porcelain]. Budapest, 1954.

DOBROVITS, A.: "Gádor István művészete" [The Art of István Gádor]. *Az Iparművészeti Múzeum évkönyvei* II [Yearbook of the Museum of Applied Arts II]. Budapest, 1955, p. 186.

FARÉ, M.: *La Céramique contemporaine.* Paris, 1953.

FEUCHTMÜLLER, R.–MRAZEK, W.: *Kunst in Österreich 1860–1918.* Vienna, 1964.

HAGGAR, R. G.: *Recent Ceramic Sculpture in Great Britain.* London, 1946.

HAGGAR, R. G.: *A Concise History of Ceramic Art.* London, 1959.

HETTES, K.–RADA, P.: *Moderne Keramik.* Prague, 1965.

HOFSTÄTTER, H. H.: *Geschichte der europäischen Jugendstilmalerei.* Cologne, 1963.

KARDOS, E.–VAYER, L.: *Mostra di Margit Kovács ceramista.* Rome, 1959.

KATONA, I.: "Modern iparművészetünk néhány kérdése" [Some Questions on Our Modern Applied Art]. *Művészettörténeti Értesítő* 4 (1970), pp. 278–280.

KATONA, I.: *Gorka Géza.* Budapest, 1971.

KOCZOGH, Á.: "The Art of Margit Kovács." *New Hungarian Quarterly*, Budapest (1970), pp. 184–185.

KONTHA, S.: "A politikai-ideológiai áramlatok hatása. (Különös tekintettel a szobrászatra.) A magyar képzőművészet a két világháború között" [The Effect of Political and Ideological Trends. With Special Regard to Sculpture. Hungarian Fine Art between the Two World Wars]. *Művészettörténeti Értesítő* 2 (1973), pp. 113–116. Offprint.

KOÓS, J.: "A Wiener Werkstätte: 1903–1932." *Művészettörténeti Értesítő* 1–2 (1968), pp. 43–53.

KOÓS, J.: "Parallele Erscheinungen in der Tätigkeit der Wiener Werkstätte und der Budapester Werkstatt." *Az Iparművészeti Múzeum Évkönyvei* VIII [Yearbook of the Museum of Applied Arts VIII], pp. 51–82.

KOÓS, J.: "Az 'Art Deco' néhány sajátossága. A magyar képzőművészet a két világháború között [Some Characteristics of Art Deco. Hungarian Fine Art between the Two World Wars]. *Művészettörténeti Értesítő* 2 (1973), pp. 138–193. Offprint.

MADSEN-TSCHUDI, S.: *The Sources of Art Nouveau.* Oslo, 1955.

MAJOR, M.: *Kovács Margit keramikusművész kiállítása* [The Exhibition of Margit Kovács, Ceramist]. Catalogue, Preface. Budapest, Műcsarnok, 1970.

MAJOR, M.: "Magyar építészet a két világháború között" [Hungarian Architecture between the Two World Wars]. *Művészettörténeti Értesítő* 2 (1973), pp. 98–109. Offprint.

Modern Hungarian Ceramics at the Royal Festival Hall. Catalogue. London, September 1963.

MUCHA, A.: *Documents décoratifs.* Paris, 1902.

OELMACHER, A.: *Kovács Margit gyűjteményes kiállítása* [Retrospective Exhibition of Margit Kovács]. Catalogue. Budapest, 1942.

OELMACHER, A.: *Kovács Margit. A gyűjteményes kiállítás katalógusa* [Margit Kovács. Retrospective Exhibition]. Catalogue. Budapest, 1953.

OELMACHER, A.: "Kovács Margit." *Művészet* VIII (1962), p. 40.

PATAKY, E.: *A Zsolnay kerámia* [Zsolnay Glazed Pottery]. Budapest, 1955.

P. BRESTYÁNSZKY, I.: *La moderna ceramica ungherese.* Faenza, 1964, pp. 130–132.

P. BRESTYÁNSZKY, I.: *Moderne ungarische Keramik.* Budapest, 1965.

P. BRESTYÁNSZKY, I.: *Ungheria (Mostra di ceramica...).* Rome, 1965.

P. BRESTYÁNSZKY, I.: *Ismerjük meg a kerámiát!* [Let's Get Acquainted with Ceramics]. Budapest, 1966.

P. BRESTYÁNSZKY, I.: "The Ceramics of István Gádor." *New Hungarian Quarterly*, vol. 6, pp. 214–218.

P. BRESTYÁNSZKY, I.: "Kovács Margitról" [About Margit Kovács]. *Művészet* XI (1970).

P. BRESTYÁNSZKY, I.: "Poézis, tradíció, modernség" [Poesy, Tradition, Modernity]. *Művészet* VII (1973).

PEVSNER, N.: *Pioneers of Modern Design.* London, 1949.

POGÁNY, F.: "Iparművészetünk a két világháború között. A magyar képzőművészet a két világháború között" [Our Applied Arts between the Two World Wars. Hungarian Fine Arts between the Two World Wars]. *Művészettörténeti Értesítő* 2 (1973), pp. 127–130.

PÓK, L.: *A szecesszió* [The Secession]. Budapest, 1972.

ROMVÁRY, F.: *I. Országos Kerámia Biennále* [First National Biennale of Ceramics]. Pécs, 1968.

RUSKIN, J.: *The Stones of Venice.* 1851–53.

WAGNER, D.: "Die Kunst der Gegenwart." *Ver Sacrum*, Vienna, III, 1900.

Wiener Werkstätte (Die). Modernes Kunsthandwerk 1903–1932. Cat. No. 49, Vienna, 1967. Öst. Museum für Angewandte Kunst.

YBL, E.: "A szecesszió jelentősége" [The Importance of the Art Nouveau]. *Emlékkönyv Lyka Károly hetvenötödik születésnapjára* [Commemorative Volume for the Seventy-fifth Birthday of Károly Lyka]. Budapest, 1944.

Major Awards and Exhibitions

1928 — 398th Group Show, Budapest. Nemzeti Szalon
1930 — Fourth International Exhibition of Applied Arts. Monza. Diploma
1930 — Christmas Exhibition of the Hungarian Society of Applied Arts
1932 — Exhibition of the Hungarian Society of Applied Arts
1933 — Fourth Triennale. Milan. Silver medal
1935 — Applied Arts Memorial Exhibition. Budapest. Diploma
1935 — World's Fair. Brussels
1935 — Retrospective Exhibition. Budapest. Tamás Gallery
1936 — Fifth Triennale. Milan. Gold medal
1936 — Exhibition of Hungarian Folk and Applied Arts. Helsinki
1937 — World Exhibition. Paris. Diploma
1937 — Exhibition of the Hungarian Society of Applied Arts. Budapest. Silver medal
1938 — Group Exhibition. Budapest
1938 — First National Exhibition of Applied Arts. Budapest. Gold medal
1938 — International Exhibition of Applied Arts. Berlin. Gold medal
1938 — Group Exhibition with István Pekáry and Lajos Erdős. Budapest. Tamás Gallery
1939 — Sixth Triennale. Milan. Silver medal
1940 — Seventh International Exhibition. Milan. Silver medal
1942 — Retrospective Exhibition. Budapest. Tamás Gallery

1944 — "Religious Art in the Home". Budapest
1948 — Retrospective Exhibition. Budapest. Fényes Adolf Gallery
1948 — The Kossuth Prize
1952 — First Exhibition of Applied Arts. Budapest
1953 — Retrospective Exhibition. Budapest. Nemzeti Szalon
1953 — Artist of Merit of the Hungarian People's Republic
1955 — Exhibition of Folk and Applied Arts in Honour of the 10th anniversary of Hungary's Liberation. First Prize
1958 — World Exhibition. Brussels. Grand Prize
1958 — Hungarian Exhibit of the Venice Biennale
1959 — Retrospective Exhibition. Rome. Hungarian Institute
1959 — International Exhibition of Ceramics. Ostende
1959 — Honoured Artist of the Hungarian People's Republic
1961 — Exhibition of Hungarian Applied Arts. Turin
1962 — Retrospective Exhibition. Budapest. Ernst Museum
1962 — Medal for Outstanding Achievements
1962 — International Exhibition of Ceramics. Prague. Silver medal
1963 — Exhibition of Modern Hungarian Ceramics. London
1965 — Fifth National Exhibition of Applied Art. Budapest. Art Gallery
1968 — Second National Biennale of Ceramics. Pécs
1970 — Retrospective Exhibition. Budapest. Art Gallery
1971 — Retrospective Exhibition. Győr
1971 — Honorary Citizen of Győr
1972 — Gold Medal for Outstanding Achievements
1973 — Pro Pest County Medal of Merit

Colour plates

St. George (see Ill. 79)

St. George Killing the Dragon (see Ill. 80) *2*

The Last Supper (see Ill. 82)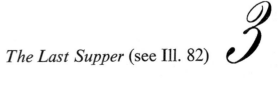

Virgin and Child (detail; see Ill. 84) 4

Pound-cake Madonna (see Ill. 7) *5*

Adam and Eve (see Ill. 85) *6*

Sisters I (see Ill. 9)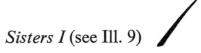

Adoration of the Magi (detail; see Ill. 86) 8

Angel-column (see Ill. 12)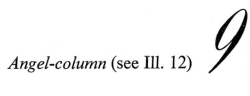

The Virgin Swaddling the Child (see Ill. 13) *10*

The Princess (see Ill. 14) *11*

St. Michael, a niche-relief (see Ill. 88) *12*

Man with Lamb (see Ill. 17) **13**

Corpus (see Ill. 19) **14**

Nursing Mother (see Ill. 20)   *15*

Nursing Mother (detail; see Ill. 20) *16*

My Mother (see Ill. 21) *17*

Proposal (see Ill. 22) *18*   *Lady* (see Ill. 23) *19*

Lady (detail; see Ill. 23) 20

"Fluctuat nec mergitur". *Jug* (see Ill. 134)   *21*

"Fluctuat nec mergitur". Jug (detail; see Ill. 134) 22

Dish with Lizard (see Ill. 135) 23

Dish with Vulture (see Ill. 136) 24

Tale (detail; see Ill. 90) **25**

Pitcher with White and Blue Flowers (see Ill. 137) *26*

Cutting the Loaf (see Ill. 25) *27*

Cutting the Loaf (detail; see Ill. 25)   28

Family Photograph Album (see Ill. 26) **29**

Man on an Ass (see Ill. 27) *30*

Betrothed Couple at the Photographer's (see Ill. 28) *31*

The Spinning Room (see Ill. 29) *32*

Margot (see Ill. 30) **33**

Stove with Wedding Scenes (see Ill. 96) *34*

Cotton Pickers (see Ill. 100) *35*

Wedding (see (Ill. 102) *36*

Swineherd (see Ill. 33) *37*

Lady Doing Her Hair (see Ill. 34) *38*

Old Shepherd (see Ill. 36) **39**

Old Shepherd (detail; see Ill. 36) *40*

Visitation (see Ill. 38) 41

Fates (see Ill. 40) 42

The Secret Tryst (see Ill. 44) 43

A Big Family (see Ill. 108) *44*

Embracing (see Ill. 109) *45*

Commemorative Dish to the 40th Wedding Anniversary of Gyula Kaesz and His Wife **46**
(see Ill. 111)

Open-work Pitcher-Girl (see Ill. 50) 47

Open-work Pitcher-Girl (detail; see Ill. 50) 48

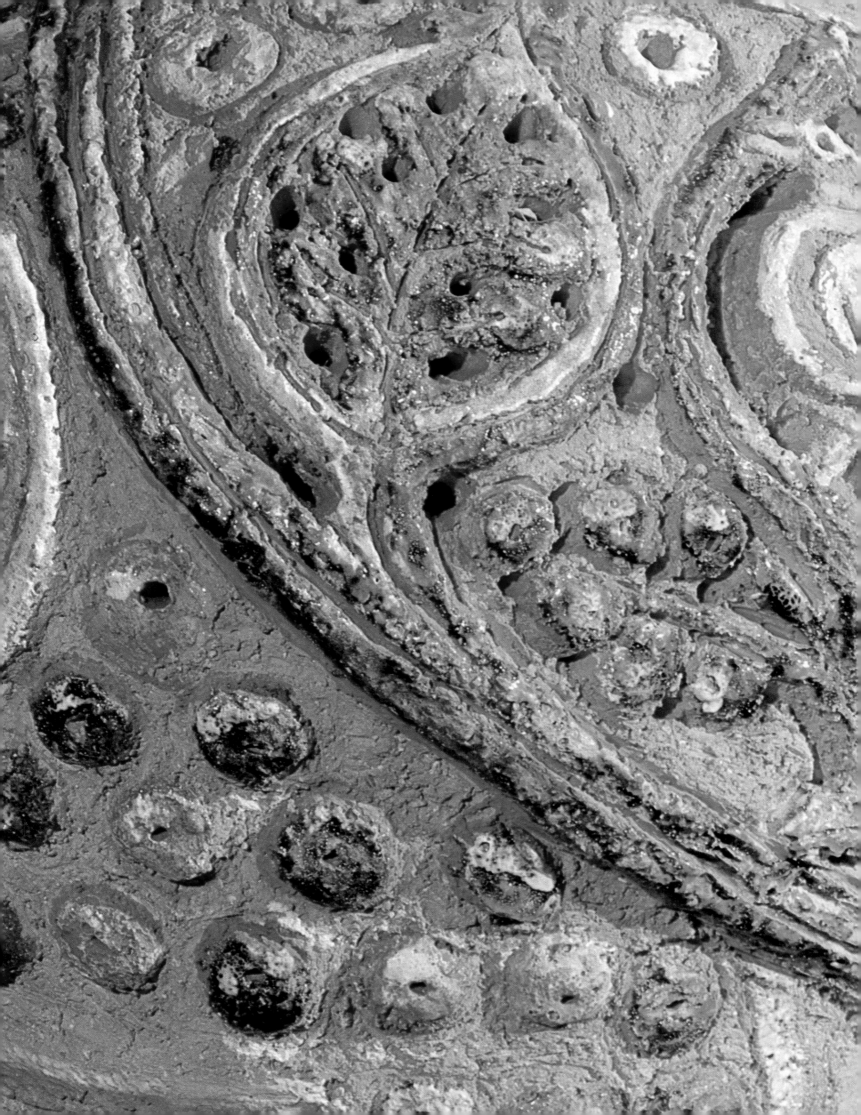

Odysseus (see Ill. 55) 49

Mother and Daughter (see Ill. 57) 50

Hommage à Szentendre (see Ill. 58) *51*

Fishermen's Wives (see Ill. 59) 52

The Father, the Son and the Ass (see Ill. 118) *53*

The Seed (see Ill. 121) **54**

Two Maidens on a Dream Ship (see Ill. 122) 55

Shepherds (detail; see Ill. 67) *56*

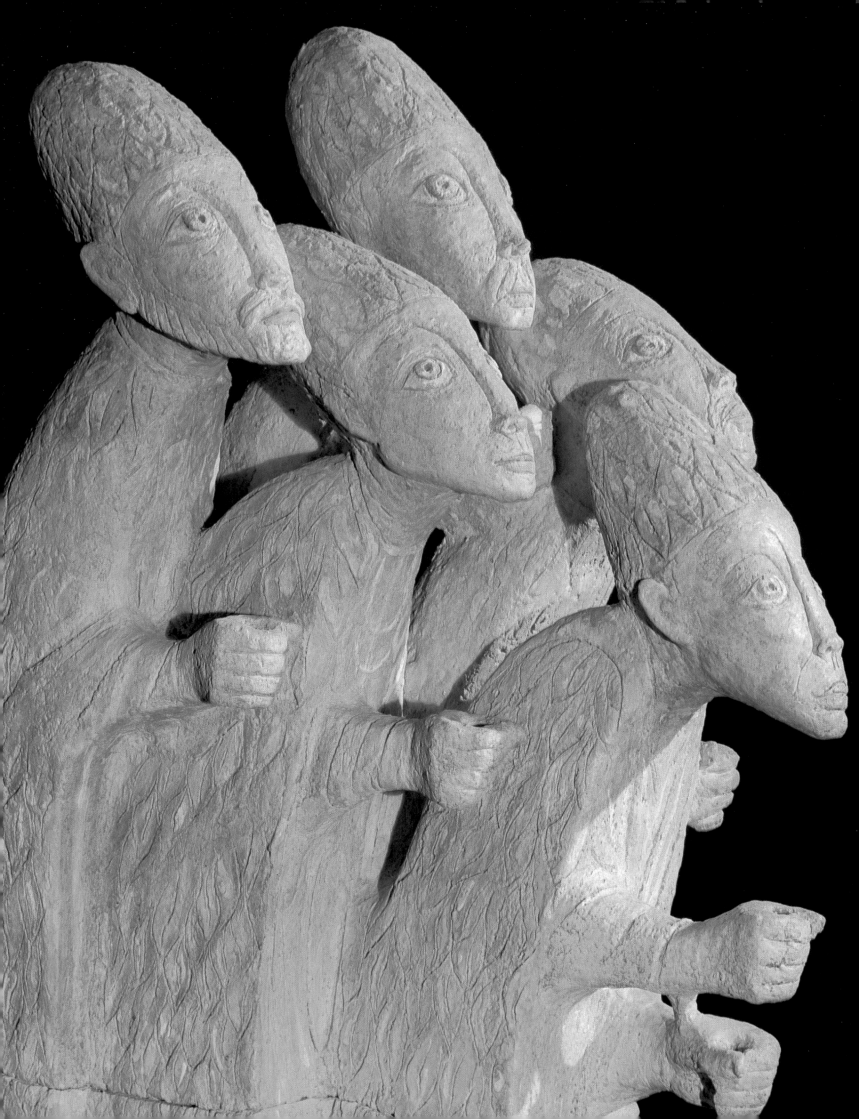

Sirens (see Ill. 69) **57**

Cantata Profana (see Ill. 125) **58**

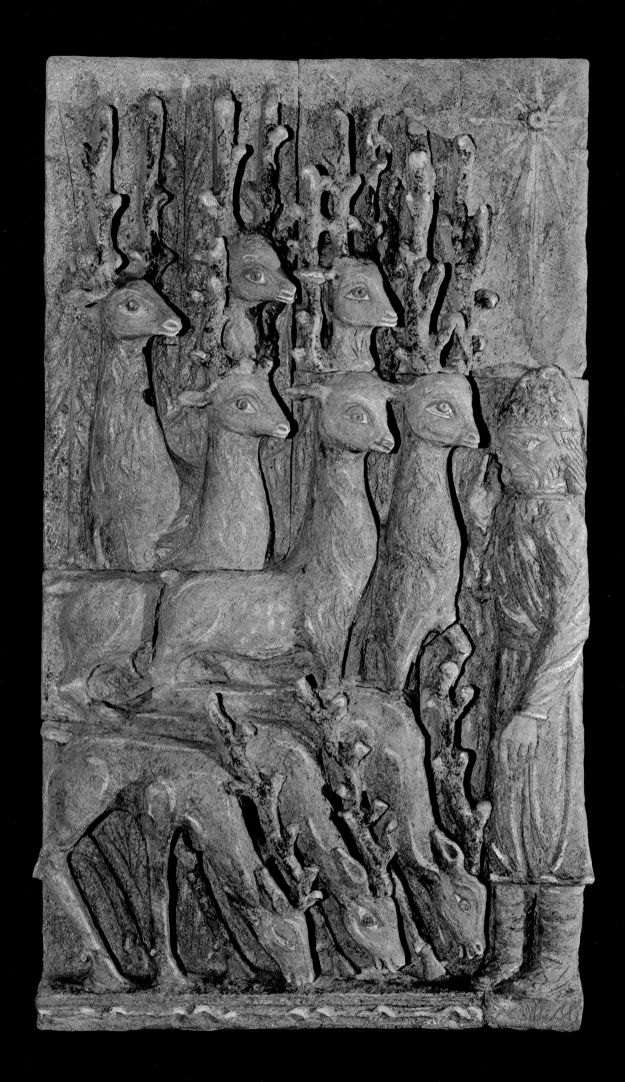

Philemon and Baucis (see Ill. 73) *59*

Philemon and Baucis (detail; see Ill. 73) *60*

The Good and the Wicked Fairy (see Ill. 76) **61**

The History of Győr, 700th Anniversary. Kazinczy after Kufstein (see Ill. 127) *62*

MEG- CSÓKOLÁ
UJOM HEGYED
S A MAGYAR
FÖLDRE NYOMÁN
E CSÓKOT

ASVÁNY · MELLETT · KÖTE · KI
HAJONK · GYŐR · KÖZE · VALA ·

KAZINCZY

The History of Győr, 700th Anniversary. Town View and Key of Győr (see Ill. 127)

Now which Is the Mother and which the Daughter? (see Ill. 77) 65

Catalogue

Those works marked in the captions "Owned by M. K." have since her death been bequested to the state and to her heirs.

*Szentendre=the permanent exhibition
of Margit Kovács's works in the former
Vastagh György House
Győr=the collection temporarily exhibited
at the Xantus János Museum,
owned by the artist*

FEMALE FIGURE WITH VASE, 1931
Terracotta with glaze
25 cm. Whereabouts unknown

LITTLE BOY IN NIGHTDRESS, 1933
Terracotta, modelled, with glaze
38 cm. Szentendre

LITTLE GIRL WITH DOLL I, 1933–34
Terracotta, modelled, with engobe painting
16 cm. Szentendre (Ill. 1)

3

YOUNG GIRL COMBING HER HAIR,
1933–34
Terracotta, modelled, with glaze
30 cm. Whereabouts unknown

LITTLE GIRL
ON THE MERRY-GO-ROUND, 1933–34
Terracotta, modelled
40 cm. Owned by M. K.

MODEST VIRGIN, c. 1935
Terracotta, modelled, antiquated
115 cm. Owned by M. K. (Ill. 4)

YOUNG APPRENTICE, c. 1934
Terracotta, modelled, antiquated
115 cm. Szentendre (Ill. 5)

GARDENERS, c. 1934
Terracotta, modelled
30 cm. Owned by M. K.

CONE-SHAPED FIGURES, c. 1934–35
Terracotta, engraved
12 cm. Owned by M. K.

MOTHER WITH HER CHILD, 1935
Terracotta, modelled, antiquated
80 cm. Szentendre

GIRL WITH LAMB, c. 1935
Terracotta, turned
38 cm. Whereabouts unknown

CAVALIER, 1936
Terracotta, turned, with engobe painting
and glaze. 41 cm. Szentendre

1

LITTLE GIRL, 1933–34
Terracotta, modelled, with glaze
signed "K M"
19 cm. Owned by M. K.

GIRL LOOKING INTO THE MIRROR,
1933–34
Terracotta, modelled, with glaze
27 cm. Szentendre (Ill. 2)

6

FLUTE-PLAYER, 1936
Terracotta, turned. 41 cm. Szentendre

FRAME FOR A TABLE CLOCK, 1936
Turned, modelled, terracotta
with coloured glazing, signed "1936"
Whereabouts unknown (Ill. 6)

GIRL PICKING FLOWERS, 1938
Terracotta, modelled
21 cm. Szentendre

POUND-CAKE MADONNA, 1938
Turned, terracotta, with engobe painting,
appliqued and engraved ornamentation,
with the inscription "Édes virágszál, Szűz Mária
— Imádkozzál értünk — K. M."
(Sweet flower, Holy Virgin, Pray for us — K.M.)
36 cm. Szentendre (Ill. 7 and colour plate 5)

4   5

PLUMP-CHEEKED GIRL, 1933–34
Chamotte clay, modelled
39 cm. Szentendre (Ill. 3)

SILLY GIRL WITH FLOWER, 1934
Terracotta, turned, with glaze
12 cm. Owned by M. K.

TWO CHILDREN, 1934
Terracotta, modelled, signed "K M"
30 cm. Owned by M. K.

2

ANGEL PLAYING THE HARP, 1940
Turned, terracotta, with engraving,
engobe painting and coloured glaze,
signed "K. M. 1940"
58 cm. Szentendre (Ill. 8)

ABYSSINIAN BOY WITH TIARA, c. 1940
Terracotta, modelled, with glaze
30 cm. Owned by M. K.

WOMAN WITH MIRROR, 1941–42
Terracotta, modelled, engraved,
with engobe painting
45 cm. Owned by M. K.

SISTERS I, 1942
Terracotta, modelled
51 cm. Győr (Ill. 9 and colour plate 7)

ST. MARGARET, c. 1942
Terracotta, modelled
142 cm. Owned by M. K.

SISTERS II, c. 1942
Terracotta, modelled
50 cm. Szentendre

ST. PETER, c. 1942
Modelled, terracotta,
with the inscription boy "*Petrus*"
92 cm. Hotel Duna-Intercontinental,
Budapest (Ill. 10)

THE GOOD SHEPHERD, 1942
Vitrified brick (clinker) turned,
with the inscription
"*Mennyből az angyal lejött hozzátok —
Pásztorok*" (See, Shepherds, an Angel
from Heaven has come down to visit you)
139 cm. Szentendre (Ill. 11)

7

9

ANGEL-COLUMN, c. 1942
Turned and modelled,
with the inscription "*Angelus, Sanctus*"
91 cm. Szentendre (Ill. 12 and colour plate 9)

8

10   11

BETHLEHEM, 1942
Turned, lost

*THE VIRGIN SWADDLING THE CHILD,
c. 1942*
Modelled, terracotta
with engraved ornamentation
31 cm. Szentendre
(Ill. 13 and colour plate 10)

LITTLE GIRL WITH DOLL II, 1942–43
Terracotta, modelled, signed "*K. M.*"
26 cm. Owned by M. K.

12

SEATED LITTLE GIRL IN A GAZE, 1942–43
Terracotta, modelled, signed "*K. M.*"
20 cm. Owned by M. K.

THE PRINCESS, 1944
Modelled clay, with glazing and engobe
painting
66 cm. Győr (Ill. 14 and colour plate 11)

13

SALOME, c. 1943–44
Terracotta, turned, with engobe painting
and glazing. 39 cm. Szentendre (Ill. 15)

168

BIG GIRL WITH SMALL PLATE, c. 1944
Terracotta, turned with glaze
50 cm. Owned by M. K.

TWO MOURNERS, c. 1944
Modelled, terracotta with engraving
and engobe painting
50 cm. Szentendre (Ill. 16)

14

16

FOUR MOURNERS, 1945–50
Terracotta, modelled, with engobe painting
and glaze and engraved ornamentation
54 cm. Szentendre

THE ADMIRABLE CATCH, 1947
Terracotta, turned and modelled, inscribed:
"*Piscatus admirabilis 1947 — K M*"
40 cm. Szentendre

UNSOPHISTICATED, 1947
Turned, terracotta with engraving,
engobe painting and glazing, signed "*K. M.
1947*". 33 cm. Szentendre (Ill. 18)

18

THERESA, 1947–48
Terracotta, turned, engraved
with engobe painting
43 cm. Owned by M. K.

CORPUS, 1948
Terracotta with engobe painting and glazing,
signed "*K M*"
120 cm. Szentendre (Ill. 19 and colour plate 14)

15

MAN WITH LAMB, 1944–45
Modelled, terracotta with engraved
ornamentation
32 cm. Szentendre (Ill. 17 and colour plate 13)

MOTHER WITH HUNGRY CHILD, 1945
Terracotta, modelled
84 cm. Owned by M. K.

17

LITTLE GIRL DRINKING, 1947
Terracotta, modelled, signed "*K. M.*"
25 cm. Owned by M. K.

19

NURSING MOTHER, 1948
Terracotta with engobe painting and glaze,
signed "*K M*". 80 cm. Szentendre
(Ill. 20 and colour plates 15, 16)

GIRL WITH CHINESE EYES, 1948
Terracotta, turned, with engobe painting
and glaze. 25 cm. Szentendre

LITTLE GIRL, 1948
Terracotta, modelled
20 cm. Owned by M. K.

MY MOTHER, 1948
Terracotta, modelled
30 cm. Szentendre
(Ill. 21 and colour plate 17)

LADY, 1949
Terracotta, modelled,
with engobe painting and glaze
56 cm. Szentendre
(Ill. 23 and colour plates 19, 20)

NOSY GIRLS, c. 1948
Terracotta, modelled
32 cm. Szentendre (Ill. 24)

MATYÓ BRIDE WITH BREAD, 1950
Terracotta, turned,
with engobe painting and glaze
110 cm. Owned by M. K.

25

22   23

LADY DONNING HER GLOVE, 1949
Terracotta, turned, engraved,
with engobe painting and glaze
50 cm. Szentendre

FIGURE WITH LAMB AND DOVE,
c. 1949–50
Terracotta, turned,
with engobe painting and glaze
107 cm. Szentendre

MOURNER, 1951
Terracotta, turned, with engobe painting
50 cm. Szentendre

WOMAN SELLING APPLES, 1952
Terracotta, turned, with glazes
42 cm. Owned by M. K.

GIRL TASTING PLUMS, 1952
Terracotta, modelled, engraved,
with engobe painting and glaze
36 cm. Owned by M. K.

20

GAZING LITTLE GIRL, 1948
Terracotta, modelled
19 cm. Owned by M. K.

21

PROPOSAL, 1948
Terracotta, turned,
with engobe painting and glaze
53 cm. Szentendre (Ill. 22 and colour plate 18)

24

CHILDREN AT THE PUPPET SHOW, 1950
Terracotta, modelled, signed "*K. M. 1950*"
27 cm. Owned by M. K.

PEASANT WOMAN WITH CHICKEN, 1950
Terracotta, modelled, engraved,
with engobe painting, signed "*K. M.*"
32 cm. Owned by M. K.

26

CUTTING THE LOAF I, 1952
Turned, terracotta, engraved,
with engobe painting and glaze,
signed "*K. M. Béke*" (Peace)
107 cm. Owned by M. K.
(Ill. 25 and colour plates 27, 28)

CUTTING THE LOAF II, 1952
Terracotta, turned, engraved, with engobe
painting and glaze, inscribed "*K. M. Béke*"
(Peace). 102 cm. Owned by M. K.

SEATED LITTLE BOY, 1952
Terracotta, modelled, signed "*K. M.*"
23 cm. Owned by M. K.

27

GIRL FEEDING CHICKEN, 1952
Terracotta, turned,
with engobe painting and glaze
51 cm. Owned by M. K.

THE FIRST LETTER "A", 1952
Terracotta, turned, engraved,
with engobe painting and glaze, signed "*K. M.*"
23 cm. Owned by M. K.

28

CHILDREN READING, 1953
Terracotta, modelled
14 cm. Owned by M. K.

FAMILY PHOTOGRAPH ALBUM, 1953
Terracotta, with engobe painting and glaze
35 cm. Szentendre
(Ill. 26 and colour plate 29)

IT LOOKS LIKE RAIN, 1953
Terracotta, turned, with engobe painting
and glaze
103 cm. Owned by M. K.

29

MOTHER FROM MEZŐKÖVESD, 1953
Terracotta, turned, with engobe painting
and glazes, signed "*K. M.*"
33 cm. Owned by M. K.

OLD MAID, 1953
Terracotta, turned, engraved,
with engobe painting and glaze
45 cm. Owned by M. K.

30

MAN ON AN ASS, 1953
Modelled, terracotta, with glazing,
signed "*K. M.*"
42 cm. Szentendre
(Ill. 27 and colour plate 30)

*BETROTHED COUPLE
AT THE PHOTOGRAPHER'S*, 1953
Turned, terracotta, with engobe painting
and glaze, signed "*K. M.*"
48 cm. Szentendre (Ill. 28 and colour plate 31)

31

THE SPINNING ROOM, 1953
Turned, terracotta, with engobe painting
and glaze, with the inscription "*A fonóban szól
a nóta*" (Sweet is the sound of songs in the
spinning room)
92 cm. Szentendre (Ill. 29 and colour plate 32)

32

33

MARGOT, 1954
Turned, terracotta, with engobe painting
and glaze, with the inscription "*Margot*"
37 cm. Szentendre
(Ill. 30 and colour plate 33)

LITTLE GIRLS PLAYING, 1956
Terracotta, turned, with engobe painting
28 cm. Owned by M. K.

LARK, 1956
Terracotta, turned, engraved,
with engobe painting and glaze
24 cm. Owned by M. K.

OLD SHEPHERD, 1958
Chamotte clay, 35 cm. Szentendre
(Ill. 36 and colour plates 39, 40)

THE RAPE OF EUROPA, 1958
Turned, terracotta, with engobe painting
42 × 45 cm. Owned by M. K. (Ill. 37)

34

36

VISITATION, 1958   38
Turned, terracotta, with engobe painting,
signed "*K. M. 1958*"
33 cm. Museum of Applied Arts, Budapest
(Ill. 38 and colour plate 41)

SUSANNAH, 1955
Turned, terracotta, with engobe painting
and glaze, with the inscription "*K. M. 1955
Zsuzsánna*"
42 cm. Owned by M. K. (Ill. 31)

RECLINING LADY, 1955
Terracotta, turned, with glaze,
signed "*K. M.*"
15 cm. Owned by M. K.

PEGASUS, 1956
Terracotta, turned, with engobe painting
and glaze, inscribed *Nevem Pegazus K. M.*
(I'm called Pegasus K. M.)
33 cm. Owned by M. K.

DRINKING BOY, 1956
Terracotta, turned
50 cm. Szentendre

LADY DOING HER HAIR, 1957
Modelled, clay with engobe painting
37 cm. Győr (Ill. 34 and colour plate 38)

"*HOW NICE TO SEE YOU AGAIN*", 1958
Terracotta, turned, with engobe painting
35 cm. Szentendre

MOURNER, TURNED, 1958
Turned, terracotta, with engobe painting
and glaze, signed "*K. M. 1958*"
34 cm. Szentendre (Ill. 39)

39

THE KISS OF JUDAS, 1956   35
Chamotte clay, engraved
49 cm. Szentendre (Ill. 32)

SALOME DANCING, 1956
Terracotta, engraved 50 cm. Owned by M. K.

SWINEHERD, 1956
Turned, terracotta, with engraving, signed "*1956*"
43 cm. Szentendre (Ill. 33 and colour plate 37)

FISHERMAN, 1958   37
Chamotte clay, modelled, engraved,
signed "*K. M.*" 48 cm. Owned by M. K.

OLD FISHERMAN, 1958
Chamotte clay, modelled engraving
44 cm. Szentendre (Ill. 35)

FATES, 1958
Turned, terracotta, with engobe painting
and glaze, inscription "*Clotho, Lachesis,
Atropos Anno 1958*"
84 cm. Owned by M. K.
(Ill. 40 and colour plate 42)

SLEEPING BOY, 1958
Chamotte clay, modelled, engraved
24 cm. Szentendre (Ill. 41)

172

THE WISE AND THE FOOLISH VIRGIN,
1958–60
Terracotta, turned, with engobe painting
45 cm. Szentendre

ON CAMELBACK, *1959*
Terracotta, turned, 40 cm. Owned by M. K.

MADONNA WITH BABE-IN-ARMS, *1959*
Terracotta, turned,
with engobe painting and glaze
70 cm. Italy, in private ownership

40

"HERO BOR", *1960*
Terracotta, turned,
with engobe painting and engraved
ornamentation, inscribed *"Bor Vitéz"*
43 cm. Szentendre

OLD LAMENT, *1960*
Terracotta, turned, engraved *"Anno 1960.
Szemeim, sírjatok, Könnyeim hulljatok,
Hogy az én arcomon Patakot mossatok. K. M."*
(Anno 1960. Let my eyes weep, my tears fall,
that you may wash my face with a stream
of sorrow. M. K.). 39 cm. Szentendre (Ill. 42)

41

THREE SISTERS, *1960*
Terracotta, turned, with engobe painting
and the inscription *"Csicsónénak három lánya,
Mind a három egy szoknyában K M. 1950"*
(Mistress Csicsó has three daughters,
With one skirt for all three, alas. K M)
28 cm. Szentendre

MOURNING I, *1960*
Burnt clay, turned, with engobe painting
44 cm. Szentendre (Ill. 43)

WOMEN'S EMANCIPATION, *1960*
Fire-clay, turned engraved
45 cm. Szentendre

42

SALOME I. *1960*
Terracotta, with engobe painting
and glazing, signed *"K M"*
60 cm. Owned by M. K.

GIRL CALLING THE HUNT, *1960*
Terracotta, turned, with engobe painting
55 cm. Szentendre

43

TROIKA, *1960*
Chamotte clay, turned, modelled
40 cm. Szentendre

MOTHER WITH CHILD, *c. 1960*
Terracotta, turned, with engobe painting
and glazing. 72 cm. Szentendre

44

WELL-TO-DO WOMAN, *c. 1960*
Terracotta, turned, with engobe painting
and glazing
36 cm. Owned by M. K.

DAYDREAMER, *1960–62*
Terracotta, turned, with engobe painting
33 cm. Szentendre

THE SECRET TRYST, *1960–62*
Terracotta, turned, with engobe painting
57 cm. Owned by M. K.
(Ill. 44 and colour plate 43)

VISITATION, *1960–62*
Terracotta, turned, with engobe painting
33 cm. Szentendre

ANGELS RESTING AFTER WORK, *1960–63*
Terracotta, turned, engraved
45 cm. Szentendre

45

SHEPHERD, *1961*
Terracotta, turned, with engobe painting
81 cm. Owned by M. K.

FERTILITY, *1961*
Fire-clay, signed *"K. M."*
70 cm. Owned by M. K.

CELESTIAL TWINS, *1961–62*
Terracotta, turned, with engobe painting
82 cm. Owned by M. K.

MEAN OLD WOMAN KNITTING SOCKS,
1961–62
Terracotta, turned, with engobe painting
33 cm. Szentendre

THE DAY OF JUDGEMENT, *1962*
Chamotte clay, turned with engraved
ornamentation and the inscription
"*Harsona*" (Trumpet)
45 × 50 cm. Szentendre (Ill. 45)

QUADRIGA, *1962*
Fire-clay, modelled, with engobe painting
40 cm. Szentendre

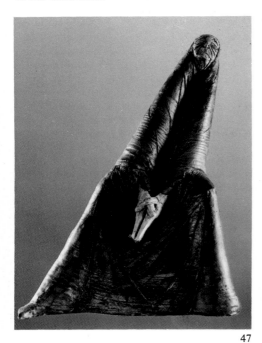

**WOMAN CARRYING
A BUNDLE OF TWIGS,** *c. 1962*
Fire-clay, turned and engraved
35 cm. Szentendre (Ill. 46)

MARKET-WOMAN, *c. 1962*
Chamotte clay, turned
25 cm. Owned by M. K.

WAITING FOR HIM, *1962–64*
Chamotte clay, modelled, with engraved
ornamentation, signed "*K. M.*"
82 cm. Szentendre

DANCING NYMPHS, *1962–65*
Terracotta, turned with engobe painting
37 cm. Szentendre

TILL DEATH DO US PART, *1964*
Terracotta, turned, with engobe painting
and engraved ornamentation
60 cm. Perished

LOVERS, *1964*
Fire-clay, modelled,
with engraved ornamentation
38 cm. Szentendre

GOD BE WITH YOU, MY SWEET LADY I,
c. 1964
Chamotte clay, turned
60 cm. Szentendre

MOTHER WITH CHUBBY CHILD, *1965*
Turned, with engobe painting and coloured
glaze, inscribed "*Anno 1965 K. M.*"
45 cm. Szentendre

MOURNING II, *1965*
Turned, terracotta, with engobe painting
44 cm. Szentendre (Ill. 47)

THE THREE KINGS, *c. 1965*
Terracotta, turned. 75 cm. Owned by M. K.

NURSING THE SICK I, *1966*
Chamotte clay, modelled
50 cm. Szentendre (Ill. 48)

IN SLEET, *1966*
Terracotta, turned, with engobe painting
40 cm. Owned by M. K. (Ill. 49)

OPEN-WORK PITCHER-GIRL, *1966*
Terracotta, turned, with engobe painting
and the inscription "*1966*". 80 cm. Szentendre
(Ill. 50 and colour plates 47, 48)

FORTUNE-TELLER GYPSYWOMAN, *1966*
Terracotta, turned, with engobe painting
110 cm. Owned by M. K.

174

WINDING THE YARN, *1966*
Chamotte clay, modelled, engraved
47 cm. Szentendre (Ill. 51)

FATIGUE, *1966*   53
Chamotte clay, turned and engraved
20 cm. Szentendre (Ill. 52)

DANCING GIRL, *1966*
Terracotta, turned, with engobe painting
50 cm. Owned by M. K.

FIGURE HOLDING A DISH, *1966*
Turned clay, with engobe painting
and engraved ornamentation
47 cm. Szentendre

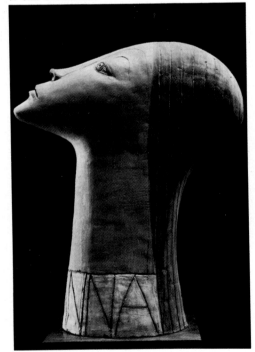

54

WITH CSILLA IN MY MIND, *c. 1966*
Terracotta, modelled
35 cm. Owned by M. K.

CENTAUR, *1966–67*
Chamotte clay, turned and engraved
42 cm. Owned by M. K.

SLUMBERING OLD MAN, *c. 1966–67*
Chamotte clay, turned and engraved
22 cm. Szentendre

DAVID, *1967*
Fire-clay mixed with clay;
etched inscription *"David"*
60 cm. Szentendre (Ill. 53)

55

JOAN, *1967*
Terracotta, turned, with engobe painting
and inscription *"Johanna K. M. 1967"*
42 cm. Owned by M. K. (Ill. 54)

ODYSSEUS, *1967*
Chamotte clay, modelled, with engobe painting,
etched *"K. M. 1967"*. 60 cm. Szentendre
(Ill. 55 and colour plate 49)

MEAN OLD WOMEN, *1967*
Chamotte clay, engobe painting
and etched inscription *"1967"*
30 × 50 cm. Szentendre (Ill. 56)

56

MOTHER AND DAUGHTER, *1968*
Fire-clay, turned and engraved
43 cm. Szentendre (Ill. 57 and colour plate 50)

HOMMAGE À SZENTENDRE, *1968*
Chamotte clay, engobe painting with inscription
"Szentendre, az édes városka K. M."
(Szentendre, delightful little town K. M.).
93 cm. Szentendre (Ill. 58 and colour plate 51)

FISHERMEN'S WIVES, *1968*
Terracotta, turned, with engobe painting
40 × 50 cm. Szentendre
(Ill. 59 and colour plate 52)

57

58

59

175

ANNUNCIATION III, 1968
Terracotta, turned, with inscription
Gloria Mária K. M.
81 × 70 cm. Szentendre (Ill. 60)

THE PATRONESS OF ONION-DOMES, 1968
Chamotte clay, turned,
signed *"1968 K. M."*
88 cm. Szentendre (Ill. 61)

60

CHESTNUT-ROASTER, 1968
Chamotte clay, engraved
60 cm. Pécs, Janus Pannonius Museum (Ill. 62)

VIGIL, 1968
Fire-clay, turned and modelled
57 × 45 cm. Szentendre (Ill. 63)

61

BIRTH, 1968
Fire-clay, turned and modelled
57 × 45 cm. Szentendre (Ill. 64)

THE WORLD IS BEAUTIFUL, 1968
Terracotta, turned, with engobe painting
100 cm. Owned by M. K.

MARRIAGE, 1968
Fire-clay, turned and engraved,
with engobe painting. 44 cm. Szentendre (Ill. 65)

62

63

DEATH, 1968
Fire-clay, turned and engraved,
with engobe painting. 44 cm. Szentendre (Ill. 66)

SUSANNAH, 1968
Fire-clay, modelled, engraved,
with engobe painting. 75 cm. Szentendre

64

SHEPHERDS, 1968
Turned, terracotta, with engobe painting
and engraving, signed *"K. M."*
101 cm. Szentendre (Ill. 67 and colour plate 56)

ANGLERS, 1968
Chamotte clay, turned and engraved,
signed *"K. M."*
48 cm. Szentendre (Ill. 68)

65

ANGEL WITH TRUMPET, 1968–69
Terracotta, turned, with coloured glaze
82 cm. Szentendre

66

SIRENS, 1968–69
Chamotte clay, turned, with engobe painting,
signed *"K. M."*
72 cm. Szentendre (Ill. 69 and colour plate 57)

FUNERAL ORATION, 1970
Fire-clay mixed with clay, turned, engraved,
with the inscription *"Látjátok, feleim..."*
(See my Brethren...)
141 cm. Szentendre (Ill. 70)

THE BUGLER, c. 1968–70   67
Terracotta, turned, engraved
91 cm. Szentendre (Ill. 71)

THEATRE, 1969
Terracotta, turned, with engobe decoration,
inscribed "1969 K. M." 80 cm. Szentendre

68

ROYAL BETROTHAL, 1969
Turned, fire-clay, with engobe painting, mosaic
and engraved ornamentation,
signed "1969 K. M." 80 cm. Szentendre (Ill. 72)

SMALL CRUCIFIX, 1969–70
Fire-clay, with etched ornamentation
45 cm. Owned by M. K.

MOTHER WITH HER CHILD, 1970
Fire-clay, turned, engraved. 45 cm. Szentendre

PHILEMON AND BAUCIS, 1970
Terracotta, turned, with engobe painting
70 cm. Szentendre
(Ill. 73 and colour plates 59, 60)

69

70   71

72

THE MAGICIAN, 1970
Terracotta, turned, with engobe painting
93 cm. Szentendre (Ill. 74)

BEGGAR-WOMAN
WITH FORGET-ME-NOT BLUE EYES, 1970
Terracotta, turned, black-and-white engobe
painting
38 cm. Szentendre (Ill. 75)

73

THE GOOD AND THE WICKED FAIRY, 1970
Turned terracotta, with engobe painting
and the inscription
"A jó tündér, a rossz tündér 1970"
(The good fairy, the wicked fairy 1970)
110 cm. Szentendre (Ill. 76 and colour plate 61)

74   75

SISTERS III, 1970
Chamotte clay, with engobe painting
and coloured glaze, inscribed "Anno 1970"
74 cm. Szentendre

THE BIRTH OF LEGENDS, 1970
Chamotte clay, turned, inscribed
"Legendák születése", signed "K. M."
94 cm. Szentendre

EPITAPH, 1970
Chamotte clay, modelled, with engraved
ornamentation, inscribed
"Legyen lelke bekötve az élet kötelékébe"
(May thy soul become a link in life's eternal
chain)
88 cm. Szentendre

SHEPHERD, c. 1970
Chamotte clay, modelled, engraved
33 cm. Szentendre

SEATED MADONNA, 1972
Terracotta, turned, with engobe painting
105 cm. I, Tárnok utca 18, Budapest

GOTHIC MADONNA, 1972
Terracotta, turned, with engobe painting,
signed *"1972 K. M."*
107 cm. Szentendre

"OH VENICE!", 1972
Chamotte clay with engobe painting and
engraving, inscription
"Oh Velence 1972. K. M."
110 cm. Szentendre

SUNDAY, 1973
Terracotta, turned, with engobe painting,
inscribed *"Vasárnap K. M."*
65 cm. Szentendre

TEST FLIGHT, 1973
Terracotta, modelled, with the inscription
"Próbarepülés"
84 cm. Owned by M. K.

*"NOW WHICH IS THE MOTHER
AND WHICH THE DAUGHTER?", 1974*
Fire-clay mixed with clay
80 cm. Owned by M. K.
(Ill. 77 and colour plate 65)

76

77

178

KNEELING WOMAN, 1928
Terracotta relief, modelled, with glaze
20 × 30 cm. Lost

PARADISE, 1929
Terracotta relief, modelled,
with coloured glaze
41 × 39 cm. Owned by M. K.

CAIN AND ABEL, 1929
Terracotta relief, modelled
36 × 25 cm. Szentendre

BOY AT THE POTTER'S WHEEL, 1929
Terracotta relief, glazed,
with the inscription "1929 K. M."
42 × 52 cm. Szentendre

JACOB'S DREAM, 1929
Terracotta relief, modelled, with the inscription
"Jákob 1929 álma"
45 × 62 cm. Owned by M. K.

MARY WITH TWO HIRED MOURNERS, 1929
Terracotta relief, modelled,
with the inscription "Mária"
40 × 25 cm. Owned by M. K.

ST. GEORGE, c. 1930
Niche-relief
40 × 25 cm. Whereabouts unknown

78

ANCIENT OCCUPATIONS, 1931
Terracotta relief, modelled,
with coloured glazes and the inscription
"Piscatus, Venatus, Pecuaria, Agricultura —
Budapest — KM 1931"
Vienna, Tourist Office (Ill. 78)

ST. FREDERICUS, c. 1931
Terracotta niche-relief, modelled,
with coloured glazes and the inscription
"Fredericus 1931"
65 × 35 cm. Owned by M. K.

ST. IMRE, c. 1931
Terracotta niche-relief, modelled
with the inscription "Szent Imre herceg"
28 × 34 cm. Owned by M. K.

FISHING BOY, 1932
Terracotta relief, with coloured glazes
and the inscription "1932 Aquam..."
40 × 35 cm. I, Ponty utca 14, Budapest

CAIN AND ABEL, 1932
Terracotta relief, modelled
25 × 36 cm. Szentendre

GIRL HOLDING ON TO A GOAT, 1933
Terracotta niche-relief, modelled, with glazes
and the inscription "Anno Domini 1933"
35 × 45 cm. Owned by M. K.

WET-NURSE, 1933–34
Terracotta relief, modelled
34 cm. Owned by M. K.

ST. ELIZABETH ALTAR, 1934
Terracotta relief, with engobe painting
and the inscription
"Árpádházi Szent Erzsébet Anno 1934"
58 × 42 cm. Perished

79

COUPLE ON A CART, 1934–35
Terracotta relief with engobe painting
Perished

ST. FLORIAN, 1935
Terracotta niche-relief, modelled,
with glazes and the inscription
"Édes Flórián, míg téged látunk, nem félünk"
(Sweet Florian, whilst we see thee, we fear not)
44 cm. Kaesz House, Szentendre

ST. FLORIAN, 1935
Terracotta niche-relief, modelled,
with glazes and the inscription
"K. M. Flórián 1935"
40 cm. XIII, Fürst Sándor utca 16, Budapest

ST. GEORGE, 1935
Terracotta relief cut in clay with engobe
and lead enamel painting and the inscription
"Sct Georgius"
36 × 40 cm. Szentendre
(Ill. 79 and colour plate 1)

ANNUNCIATION I, 1935
Terracotta relief, engraved, modelled,
with glazes and signed "K. M. 1935"
14 × 15 cm. Szentendre

ICON MADONNA, c. 1935
Terracotta, flat-relief with engobe painting
and glazes, inscribed "Mária K M"
39 cm. Owned by M. K.

80

RELIEF WITH ANGEL
AND LAMB IN A DISH, c. 1935
Terracotta, turned, modelled, with glaze
32 cm. Szentendre

"THE PEACOCK ALIGHTED", c. 1935
Terracotta relief
150 × 100 cm.
The façade of V, Vármegye utca 15,
Budapest

THE HOLY FAMILY, c. 1935
Terracotta, with engobe painting
Whereabouts unknown

ST. GEORGE KILLING THE DRAGON, 1936
Terracotta relief, modelled,
with engobe and glazed painting
62 × 42 cm. Szentendre
(Ill. 80 and colour plate 2)

SIGNS OF THE ZODIAC, c. 1936
Terracotta relief, engraved, with engobe
painting and glazes (each pillar 220 cm.
and back of the bench 47 × 47 cm. each)
In the foyer of I, Kosciuszkó Tádé u. 14,
Budapest

THE RELIEF OF THE PULPIT
OF THE ROMAN CATHOLIC CHURCH
AT KOMÁROM, 1937
Terracotta flat relief, with engobe glaze
and engraving
Perished

ST. ELIZABETH, 1937
Terracotta, modelled
At the former Ügyész utca 6, Budapest
Perished

"TO THE OLD POST-HOUSE", 1937
Terracotta relief, modelled,
with glazes and the inscription
"K M 1937 A 'Régi Postaház'-hoz"
60 × 180 cm. The façade of
V, Régiposta utca 13, Budapest

*BUDAPEST, THE QUEEN
OF THE DANUBE, 1937*
Mural, clinker, with coloured glazes
600×400 cm. Perished. Remnant at IBUSZ,
V, Roosevelt tér 5, Budapest

81

*THE HISTORY OF THE MAIL SERVICE,
1937*
Terracotta mural with glazes and the inscription
"K. M. Anno Domini 1937"
Formerly at XIV, Cházár utca, Budapest
Perished

LET'S RESPECT WOMEN! 1937
Terracotta mural, with glaze
Perished

82

*THE SMALL ALTAR OF ST. CHARLES
OF BORROMEO, 1937*
Terracotta relief, modelled, with glazes
and the inscription
*"Borromei Szent Károly, imádkozzál érettünk —
1937 K. M."*
(St. Charles of Borromeo, pray for us)
84×42 cm. Győr. Perished

LACE-BIRD, 1937
Terracotta relief, engraved, with earth paints
and glazes and the inscription
*"K M — Páros madár a gilicemadár,
Párja nélkül még a vízre se jár"*
(Turtle-doves will drink not of clear water—
If their true helpmates be flown away)
35×33 cm. Perished

83

ORNAMENTAL STOVE, 1938
Terracotta, with engraving and glazes,
signed *"Anno 1938"* (made for the First National
Exhibition of Applied Arts, Berlin, 1938)
In a private collection, Milan (Ill. 81)

*THE FLOOR OF THE BAPTISMAL
AND HEROES' CHAPEL
OF THE VÁROSMAJOR CHURCH, 1938*
Terracotta, with painted glazes. Perished

84

ST. FRANCIS, 1938
Terracotta, with engobe painting
II, Csalogány utca 39, Budapest. Perished

SAINTS OF THE HOUSE OF ÁRPÁD, 1938
Row of five niche-reliefs, terracotta,
with engobe painting and with the inscription
on the two central pilasters: *"1938"*
70×43 cm. each. Owned by M. K.

THE LAST SUPPER, 1938
Mural, terracotta embedded in cast stone,
with engobe painting, glazes, and engraved
ornamentation
120×87 cm. Szentendre
(Ill. 82 and colour plate 3)

85

ANGEL, 1938
Moulded, terracotta with glazes
(decoration of a stove)
35×70 cm. Szentendre

86

ANNUNCIATION II, 1938
Mural, terracotta embedded in cast stone,
engraved, with earth paints and glazes,
signed *"1938 K M"*
56×82 cm. Szentendre (Ill. 83)

MARK—LUKE, 1938
Mural, clinker, painted with glazes
90 × 107 cm. Owned by M. K.

VIRGIN AND CHILD, 1938–42
Terracotta with engraving, engobe and enamel
painting, the inscription "*Mária Jézus K M*"
41 × 40 cm. Szentendre
(Ill. 84 and colour plate 4)

**THE ENTRANCE
OF ST. IMRE'S CHURCH AT GYŐR,
1939–40**
Terracotta, with engobe painting, engraved
Győr

87

ADAM AND EVE, c. 1939–40
Terracotta, modelled,
with glazes (column-casing)
150 cm. V, Vármegye utca 15, Budapest

THE MIRACULOUS CATCH, 1940
Terracotta on canvas, with engobe painting
and the inscription "*Andreas Petrus Jesus —
Anno Domini 1940. Csodálatos halfogás*"
33 × 46 cm. Szentendre

APOSTLES PETER AND PAUL, c. 1940
Round clinker relief with glazes
40 cm. Szentendre

**GOLDEN-FRAMED ICON MADONNA,
1940–41**
Terracotta mural, painted with glazes
and with the inscription "*Mária K M*"
60 × 60 cm. Owned by M. K.

ADAM AND EVE, 1941
Relief in terracotta, modelled,
signed "*K M 1941*"
40 × 63 cm. Szentendre
(Ill. 85 and colour plate 6)

ADORATION OF THE MAGI, 1942
Mural, terracotta with engraving,
engobe painting and glazes, signed "*1942 K M*"
63 × 180 cm. Szentendre
(Ill. 86 and colour plate 8)

GOLGOTHA, 1942
Terracotta relief with engobe painting
and engraved ornamentation
76 × 128 cm. Szentendre

BETHLEHEM, 1942
Terracotta, turned. Lost.

**MAY GOD GRANT WINE,
WHEAT AND PEACE, 1942**
Relief in terracotta, engraved with glazed
ornamentation, signed "*1942 K M*"
115 × 136 cm. Owned by M. K. (Ill. 87)

SLEEPING BEAUTY, 1942   88
Terracotta mural with engobe painting
125 × 140 cm. Owned by M. K.

WOMAN'S HEAD WITH CARNATION, 1942
Terracotta, engraved, with engobe painting
47 cm. Owned by M. K.

FISHING, HUNTING, 1942
Flat terracotta relief with engobe painting
and glazes, and with the inscription
"*Halászat — Vadászat K M 1942*"
80 × 115 cm. In the lobby of II, Bimbó út 11,
Budapest

**WOMAN'S HEAD ENGRAVED
IN INTAGLIO, 1942**
Terracotta, engraved, signed "*K M 1942*"
132 × 203 cm. Owned by M. K.

89

THE GUITAR PLAYER, 1942
Terracotta, modelled, with engobe painting
22 cm. Owned by M. K.

APOSTLES PETER AND PAUL, 1942
Clinker, painted with glazes, inscribed
"*Péter Pál K M*"
27 cm. Owned by M. K.

PIOUS GIRLS WITH CANDLES, 1942
Terracotta, painted and glazed,
signed "*K. M.*"
60 × 41 cm. Owned by M. K.

ST. MICHAEL, a niche relief, 1944
Terracotta, turned, modelled, with engobe
painting, glazed; the inscription reads
"*Paradisi Michael prepositus*"
32 cm. Owned by M. K.
(Ill. 88 and colour plate 12)

SAINT WITH LAMB AND BIRD, c. 1944
Terracotta relief, engraved, antiqued
32 × 48 cm. Szentendre

**SKETCH FOR AN AQUINCUM MURAL,
c. 1945–50**
Terracotta with engobe painting, inscribed
"*Aquincumról énekelek*" (I sing of Aquincum)
12 × 25 cm. Szentendre

**MAY FIRST, DETAIL OF A MURAL,
c. 1946**
Terracotta with glazes
102 × 115 cm. Ministry of Education, Budapest

90

NORN, 1947–48
Mural, painted and glazed, signed "*K M*"
30 × 50 cm. Owned by M. K.

ST. LUKE, 1948
Terracotta, mural, glazed and inscribed
"*Lukács — Anno Domini 1948*"
20 × 30 cm. Szentendre

"FAIR MAIDEN, JÚLIA", 1948
Terracotta relief, engraved, with engobe
painting and the inscription
"*Júlia szép leány — Egykoron kimőne —
Búzavirág szödni — A búzamezőkre —
Anno 1948*" (Once did she go—
fair maiden Júlia—To gather blue cornflower
—In wheat fields of gold)
43 × 49 cm. Szentendre

GIRL WITH LILY AND LAMB, 1948
Terracotta, engraved and painted with glazes,
signed *A Toi K M*
30 × 62 cm. Owned by M. K.

MAP OF LAKE BALATON, 1950
Terracotta mural, painted with glazes
and engraved
240 × 260 cm. The hall of the South
Railway Station, Budapest

POOL OF A FOUNTAIN, c. 1950
Terracotta, painted with glazes
250 cm. Úttörő és Ifjúsági Áruház
(Pioneer Department Store), Budapest

95

91

WOOD-CUTTER, 1949
Terracotta relief, painted with glazes
55 cm. Owned by M. K.

93

PEASANT WOMAN BINDING
HER KERCHIEF, c. 1950
Painted in Mettlach tiles with glaze
40 × 30 cm. Owned by M. K. (Ill. 89)

GIRL WITH WHEAT STALK, c. 1950
Mettlach tiles, painted with glazes and with
the inscription "Ágas búza K M"
80 × 180 cm. Owned by M. K.

WINE HARVEST, c. 1950
Terracotta mural, engraved "1951"
49 × 17.5 cm. Owned by M. K.

GIRL FEEDING A PIGEON, 1950–51
Terracotta, painted with glazes
26 × 62 cm. Owned by M. K. (Ill. 91)

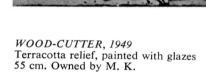

96

92

RIDERS, 1949
Relief, clinker, painted with glazes
55 cm. Owned by M. K.

MAP OF HUNGARY, 1950
Mettlach tiles, painted with glazes
and inscribed "Salve Hungaria 1950"
800 × 260 cm. Hegyeshalom railway station

94

TALE, c. 1950
Mettlach mural, glazed, inscribed
"Mese K M"
95 × 65 cm. Szentendre
(Ill. 90 and colour plate 25)

AM I NOT PRETTY? 1951
Mural, terracotta embedded in artificial stone,
engraved, with engobe painting and glazes,
inscription "Szépséges virágszál" (Beauteous
flower)
80 × 120 cm. Owned by M. K.

RELIEF WITH DOVE OF PEACE, 1951
Terracotta, turned, modelled,
with glaze and the inscription
"Éljen az élet — Éljen a béke — 1951"
(Long live life—long live peace)
30 cm. Owned by M. K.

MEAL IN THE MEADOW, 1951
Terracotta mural glazed, with engobe painting
signed "*K M*"
70×98 cm. Owned by M. K. (Ill. 92)

TURNING THE WHEEL, c. 1951
Terracotta mural with glaze and engobe
painting. 62×80 cm. Szentendre

GIRL TYING A SHEAF OF WHEAT, 1952
Terracotta relief, painted with glaze
40×40 cm. Owned by M. K.

EGG-PAINTER, 1952
Terracotta niche-relief, turned, modelled,
with engobe painting and glazes
31 cm. Owned by Mrs. L. Biró

DOVE OF THE HOLY GHOST, 1952
Terracotta relief, with glaze
7 cm. Owned by M. K.

HOMEWARDS, 1952
Mural on tiles, painted and glazed,
signed "*K M*"
50×71 cm. Owned by M. K. (Ill. 94)

BUDAI NAGY ANTAL, 1952
Terracotta mural, engraved, with engobe
painting and glaze, inscribed
"*Budai Nagy Antal — 1437 K M*"
80×80 cm. County Seat, Székesfehérvár

FOLK DANCE GROUP REHEARSING, 1952
Terracotta mural, engraved, with engobe
painting and glazes, inscribed
"*Próbál a népi tánccsoport K M*"
240 × 240 cm. Budapest. (Ill. 95)
Owned by the Hungarian Ministry of Foreign
Affairs, Budapest

97

APPLE PICKING, 1952
Mural on tiles, painted and glazed,
signed "*K M*"
120×160 cm. Owned by M. K. (Ill. 93)

99

101

98

100

183

HERO JOHN, 1952
Mural, Mettlach tiles, painted with glazes,
inscribed "*K M Petőfi Sándor János vitéz
1844*"
240 × 100 cm. Dunaújváros

102

STOVE WITH WEDDING SCENES, 1953
Terracotta, painted with glazes, Szentendre
(Ill. 96 and colour plate 34)

SINGERS, 1953
Terracotta relief, signed "*K M 1953*"
80 × 40 cm. Szentendre (Ill. 97)

104

WINE HARVEST WITH CARRIAGE, 1953
Terracotta mural, painted with glazes
on Mettlach tiles, signed "*K M Szüret*"
100 × 150 cm. Owned by M. K. (Ill. 98)

SMELTER, 1953
Terracotta relief with engobe painting
70 × 90 cm. Parád Glassworks

DRESSING THE BRIDE, 1953
Mural, terracotta embedded in artificial stone,
with engobe painting and glazes, with
inscription: "*Menyasszony leszek,
Annak is pedig, A legszebb leszek*"
(I am going to be a bride, the most beautiful
of all), signed "*K M*"
102 × 118 cm. Owned by M. K. (Ill. 99)

GIRL AT THE POTTER'S WHEEL, 1953
Terracotta mural with engobe painting
and glazes
50 × 50 cm. Szentendre

COTTON PICKERS, 1955
Terracotta relief, engraved, with engobe
painting and glazes with inscription:
"*Gyapotszedők K M*"
51.5 × 77.5 cm. Győr
(Ill. 100 and colour plate 35)

FLOWER-SONG, 1955
Terracotta mural with engobe painting
and glazes, engraved, inscribed
"*1955 K M Virágének*"
199 × 80 cm. Owned by M. K.

MATYÓ FAMILY, 1955
Terracotta mural, engraved, with engobe
painting and glazes
78 × 23 cm. Museum of Applied Arts,
Budapest

106

105

GATHERING GRAPES, 1953
Terracotta relief with engobe painting
39 × 39 cm. Owned by M. K.

THE SEASONS, 1953
Terracotta niche-relief with engobe painting
and glazes. Inscribed
"*Tavasz, nyár, ősz, tél*"
(Spring, summer, autumn, winter)
260 × 60 cm. Budapest Museum of History

GLASS-BLOWER, 1953
Terracotta relief, signed "*K M*"
70 × 90 cm. Culture Centre of the Parád
Glassworks

103

ROSE OF SÁRKÖZ, 1953
Terracotta mural, engraved, with engobe
painting and glazes, inscribed
"*Sárköz rózsája*"
33 × 33 cm. Owned by M. K.

PEASANT WEDDING, 1955
Mural, terracotta, engraved, with engobe
painting and glazes, signed "*K M*"
180 × 129 cm. Szentendre (Ill. 101)

WEDDING, 1955
Terracotta relief, modelled
87 × 103 cm. Szentendre
(Ill. 102 and colour plate 36)

GIRLS WITH LACE VEILS, 1955
Terracotta mural, engraved, with engobe
painting and glazes
63 × 47 cm. Szentendre (Ill. 103)

WINE HARVEST, 1955
Terracotta relief, modelled, with glazes
75 × 120 cm. Museum of Applied Arts,
Budapest

184

MERRY-MAKING IN THE VILLAGE, 1958
Terracotta mural, engraved, with glazes
400×200 cm. November 7 Thermal Plant,
Inota

"HEY, FISHERMEN, FISHERMEN..." 1958
Relief, chamotte clay, modelled
64×100 cm. Owned by M. K.

111

"HERO BOR", 1955
Terracotta niche-relief, turned, modelled, with
engobe painting and glaze and the inscription
*"Bor vitéz ül jó lovára — Isten hozzád
édes hölgyem"* (Hero Bor sits astride his horse
—God be with you gentle lady), signed
"K M"
37 cm. Szentendre

WINE HARVEST IN BADACSONY, 1955
Mural, Mettlach tiles, painted with glazes
200×300 cm. VIII, Dienes László utca 2,
Magyar Építőművészek Szövetsége
(Association of Hungarian Architects)

MEDIEVAL GRAPE HARVEST, 1956
Terracotta mural, engraved, painted with
glazes, signed *"K M"*
150×250 cm. Balatonfüred,
State Wine-cellars (Ill. 104)

BELLE OF THE VILLAGE, 1956
Terracotta flat-relief, engraved, with engobe
painting and glaze, inscribed
"K M — Falu szépe"
40×44 cm. Owned by M. K.

108

*SLEEPING MOTHER EARTH
AND THE FOUR SEASONS, 1959*
Terracotta relief, with engobe painting
150×100 cm. Geneva, World
Meteorological Organization (Ill. 105)

"OLD BALLAD..." 1959
Terracotta relief, engraved, with glazes,
and the inscription: *"Vitézek, mi lehet
e széles föld felett — Szebb dolog az végeknél"*
(Valients, what could compare on this round
earth—With the borderlands of gallantry)
signed *"K M"*. 66.5×48 cm. Owned by M. K.

GAMES, 1959
Terracotta mural, with painted glazes
100×200 cm. Ministry of Education,
Budapest

107

109

110

THE METEOROLOGIST, 1960
Terracotta relief, modelled, with engobe
painting and the inscription

112

113

114

"OMI 1860–1960"
140 × 135 cm. Országos Meteorológiai
Intézet (National Meteorological Institute),
Budapest

115

PICKING FRUIT, 1960
Mural, clinkers in intaglio, painted with glaze
140 × 135 cm. Owned by M. K.

116

"TWO GIRLS WENT TO PICK FLOWERS",
1961
Terracotta relief, engraved, modelled, with
engobe painting and glazing, with inscription:
"Elment a két lány virágot szedni"
114 × 149 cm. Szentendre, and a variant
at the Museum of Applied Arts,
Budapest (Ill. 106)

IN REMEMBRANCE OF THINGS PAST, 1961
Mural, terracotta, painted with glazes
and inscribed *"Eltűnt idők nyomában"*
150 × 120 cm. Blood-donor Headquarters,
Budapest

117

MAN AND WORK, 1961
Relief in chamotte clay, with
open-work prominent moulding
800 cm. Turin, Centre International
du Travail (Ill. 107)

118

119

120

123

MARKET, 1961
Terracotta relief, modelled, inscribed
"*Almát vegyenek, halat tessék, Halvásár Anno 1961*" (Buy apples, buy fish, Fishmarket Anno 1961) and signed "*K M*"
89 × 66 cm. Szentendre

125

MISTRESS RÉBÉK, 1961
Flat-relief, terracotta, engraved, with the inscription "*Fennakadsz, te szép betyár, Hess, madár, Madár mondja: kár, Rebi néni, hess — K M*" (You'll hang from the gallows, handsome rogue, Shoo, shoo, bird, shoo, Bird says you have it coming, Mistress Rébék, shoo)
110 × 34 cm. Owned by M. K.

121

122

124

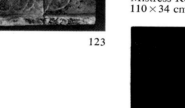

A BIG FAMILY, 1962
Terracotta mural, modelled, signed "*K M 1962*"
110 × 120 cm. Szentendre
(Ill. 108 and colour plate 44)

126

FEAST, 1963
Terracotta relief, with engobe painting
and glaze
24 × 24 cm. Szentendre

EMBRACING, 1964
Relief in clinker, with engraved ornamentation,
glazed
18 × 36 cm. Owned by M. K.
(Ill. 109 and colour plate 45)

ANGEL WATCHING FOR A SECRET, 1967
Relief, in terracotta, modelled, with engobe
painting and glazing, with inscription:
"Titkot leső angyal"
85 × 100 cm. Szentendre (Ill. 116)

WINE HARVEST, 1968
Chamotte clay, with engraved, ornamentation,
modelled, engraved, and inscribed "1968"
150 × 120 cm. Csávoly

"IN BLUE WOODS
AND GREEN FIELDS..." 1969
Relief, in chamotte clay, modelled, engobe
painting and glazes, with inscription
"Kék erdőben, zöld mezőben sétál egy madár
K M" (In blue woods and green fields a little
bird is walking)
76 × 152 cm. Szentendre (Ill. 123)

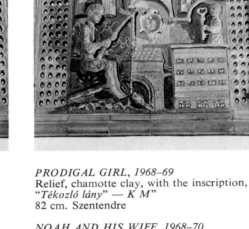

127

DREAMING—THE SHEPHERD
AND HIS FLOCK, 1965
Relief in chamotte clay,
signed "K. M. Anno 1965"
130 × 95 cm. Szentendre (Ill. 110)

IN THE WOODS, 1965
Terracotta relief, modelled, with engobe
painting and glaze, signed "K M"
740 × 100 cm. Home for Handicapped
Children, Budapest

COMMEMORATIVE DISH
TO THE 40TH WEDDING ANNIVERSARY
OF GYULA KAESZ AND HIS WIFE, 1965
Niche-relief, turned, modelled, glazed,
with inscription:
"Ily sok év a házastársak életét eggyé kovácsolta
— Az ütéseket a sors adta hozzá L K —
K GY 1925–1965–40" (Long Years welded
the lives of the couple—fate added the blows)
54 cm. Szentendre (Ill. 111 and colour plate 46)

PAGAN GROVE, 1965
High relief in chamotte clay, with engobe
painting. 97 × 83 cm. Szentendre (Ill. 112)

BE GOOD! 1966
Terracotta niche-relief, modelled,
with glaze. 36 × 50 cm. Owned by M. K.

NURSING THE SICK II, 1966
Relief in terracotta, etched, with engobe
painting, signed "Anno 1966 — K M"
81 × 94 cm. Szentendre (Ill. 113)

EXPULSION FROM PARADISE, 1967
Relief in terracotta with engobe painting,
signed "KM 1967 — Jaj Istenem" (My God)
120 × 106 cm. Szentendre (Ill. 114)

LIFE AND DEATH, 1967
Relief in chamotte clay, modelled,
signed "Élet és halál K M"
80 × 105 cm. Szentendre (Ill. 115)

PRODIGAL GIRL, 1968–69
Relief, chamotte clay, with the inscription,
"Tékozló lány" — K M"
82 cm. Szentendre

NOAH AND HIS WIFE, 1968–70
Niche-relief in chamotte clay with engobe
painting, signed "Noé, Noéné, Ararát, K M"
(Noah, his wife, Ararat)
42 × 45 cm. Szentendre (Ill. 117)

THE FATHER,
THE SON AND THE ASS, 1968–70
Niche-relief in terracotta, turned modelled,
glazed
54 cm. Szentendre (Ill. 118 and colour plate 53)

NOCTURNAL MAGIC OF THE FOREST,
1969
Relief in fire-clay, modelled, with engobe
painting
83 × 126 cm. Szentendre (Ill. 119)

THE DANCE OF SALOME, 1969
Relief in chamotte clay, with engobe painting,
glazed, signed "1969"
139 × 98 cm. Owned by M. K. (Ill. 120)

THE SEED, 1969
Relief, in chamotte clay, with engobe painting
and the inscription "A mag",
signed "K M 1969"
51.5 × 77.5 cm. Owned by M. K.
(Ill. 121 and colour plate 54)

TWO MAIDENS ON A DREAM SHIP, 1969
Relief, in terracotta, modelled, with
inscription "Két hajadon álomhajón"
155 × 143 cm. Győr
(Ill. 122 and colour plate 55)

OLD PEOPLE FEASTING IN SILENCE,
1969–70
Relief in terracotta, modelled, engobe painting,
with inscription "Öregek csöndes lakomája, K M"
106 × 150 cm. Szentendre (Ill. 124)

CANTATA PROFANA, 1969–70
Bas-relief, chamotte clay, modelled, with
engobe painting, signed "K M"
77 × 142 cm. Szentendre.
(Ill. 125 and colour plate 58)

AFFINITY, 1970
Relief, chamotte clay
73 cm. Szentendre (Ill. 126)

PIOUS GIRLS WITH CANDLESTICKS, 1971
Relief, chamotte clay, with engobe painting
and engraved ornamentation
77 × 55 cm. Szentendre

RELIEF OF SZÉKESFEHÉRVÁR, 1972
Relief, chamotte clay, with engobe painting
and glaze. 150 × 120 cm. Székesfehérvár

THE HISTORY OF GYŐR;
700TH ANNIVERSARY, 1973
Series of reliefs in terracotta, ten sections,
modelled, with engobe painting and engraved
ornamentation. 150 × 130 cm.
Győr, Hall of the Móra Ferenc Primary
School
(Ill. 127 and colour plates 62, 63, 64)
Title of each section:
St. Stephen, Koppány
Nameless Chronicler
Turkish Battles
Kazinczy after Kufstein (colour plate 62)
Town View and Key of Győr (colour plate 63)
Visit of Sándor Petőfi (colour plate 64)
Reconstruction
In memoriam Radnóti
A Quotation from Kosztolányi
Árpád's Entry

BLACK AND YELLOW CUP, *1928*
Terracotta, turned, with glaze
Whereabouts unknown

BLUE VASE WITH YELLOW GRAPES, *1928*
Terracotta, turned, with glaze
Whereabouts unknown

BLUE VASE WITH FIGURE RELIEFS, *1928*
Terracotta, turned, with glaze
Whereabouts unknown

CANDLESTICK WITH BLUE HANDLE, *1928*
Terracotta, turned, with glaze
Whereabouts unknown

BIRD-SHAPED CANDLESTICK, *1928*
Terracotta, turned, with glaze
Whereabouts unknown

BLUE DISH WITH RELIEF, *1928*
Terracotta, turned, with glaze
Whereabouts unknown

VASE WITH STAGS, *1928*
Terracotta, turned, with glaze
Whereabouts unknown

CANDLESTICK
WITH THREE ANIMAL FIGURES, *1928*
Terracotta, turned, with glaze
Whereabouts unknown

THREE-BRANCHED CANDLESTICK
WITH TWO ANIMALS, *1928*
Terracotta, turned, with glaze
Whereabouts unknown

DUCK-SHAPED CANDLESTICK, *1928*
Terracotta, turned, with glaze
Whereabouts unknown

LITTLE MAN HOLDING A FRUIT DISH,
1928
Terracotta, turned, with glaze
Lost

LION-SHAPED DISH, *1928*
Terracotta, turned, with glaze
Whereabouts unknown

ROOSTER-SHAPED DISH, *1928*
Terracotta, turned, with glaze
Whereabouts unknown

STAG-SHAPED CANDLESTICK
WITH FOUR BRANCHES, *1930*
Terracotta, turned, with glaze
Whereabouts unknown

HOLY-WATER BASIN, *1930*
Terracotta, turned, with glaze
Whereabouts unknown

MARY-JUG, *c. 1933*
Terracotta, turned, with engobe painting
37 cm. Whereabouts unknown

TWO-BRANCHED CANDLESTICK, *1933–35*
Terracotta, turned, with engobe painting
and glaze
15 cm. Whereabouts unknown

PITCHER, *1935*
Terracotta, turned, engraved, with engobe
painting
25 cm. Whereabouts unknown

PITCHER WITH ADAM AND EVE, *1935*
Terracotta, turned and painted
Whereabouts unknown

128

PITCHER WITH THE VIRGIN, *1935*
Terracotta, turned and painted
Whereabouts unknown

STAG-SHAPED PITCHER
WITH BRAIDED HANDLE, *1935–36*
Terracotta, turned, with glaze
22 cm. Owned by M. K.

129

"*IN BLUE WOODS
AND GREEN FIELDS...*", *1936*
Jug, terracotta, turned, with glaze, inscription:
"*Kék erdőben, zöld mezőben sétál egy madár —
— KM — 1936*" (In blue woods
and green fields a little bird is walking)
35 cm. Owned by M. K. (Ill. 128)

"*VANITATUM VANITAS*"
MIRROR-FRAME WITH TWO
CANDLESTICKS, *1936*
Terracotta, turned, engraved, painted with
glazes, signed "*Vanitatum vanitas 1936 KM*"
43 cm. Szentendre (Ill. 129)

DISH WITH LACE-BIRD, *1936*
Terracotta, turned, with engobe painting,
signed "*K M 1936*"
30 cm. Owned by M. K.

DISH WITH GRIFFIN, *1936*
Terracotta, turned, with engobe painting
and glaze
31 cm. Szentendre

FLAT PITCHER, *1936*
Terracotta, turned, with engobe painting
25 cm. Owned by M. K.

JUG WITH MOULDED ROOSTER, *1937*
Terracotta, turned, with engobe painting
19 cm. Owned by M. K.

PITCHER WITH ROOSTER, *1937–38*
Terracotta, turned, with glaze
20 cm. Owned by M. K.

LARGE PITCHER, *1938*
Terracotta, turned, engraved,
with engobe painting
70 cm. Szentendre

ST. GEORGE–ST. MICHAEL PITCHER,
1938
Terracotta, turned, engraved,
with engobe painting and the inscription
"*St. Georgius–St. Michael*"
56 cm. Szentendre

THE FOUR EVANGELISTS I:
THE BULL (LUKE), *1938*
Terracotta, turned, with engobe painting
and inscription "*Lucas*"
37 cm. Szentendre

130

THE FOUR EVANGELISTS II:
THE LION (MARK), *c. 1938*
Terracotta, turned, with engobe painting,
signed "*K M*"
33 cm. Szentendre

THE FOUR EVANGELISTS III:
THE RAM (MATTHEW), c. 1938
Terracotta, turned, with engobe painting,
signed "K M"
42 cm. Szentendre

GOBLET WITH FLOWERS AND HANDLE,
1940
Terracotta, turned, with engobe painting
25 cm. Owned by M. K.

PIGEON, 1940–43
Terracotta, turned, with engobe painting
15 cm. Szentendre (Ill. 131)

135

131

THE FOUR EVANGELISTS IV:
THE EAGLE (JOHN), c. 1938
Terracotta, turned, with engobe painting,
signed "K M"
42 cm. Szentendre

DISH WITH ONION-DOME, 1939
Terracotta, turned, engraved,
with engobe painting
23 cm. Owned by M. K.

133

FISH, 1940–45
Terracotta, turned, with engobe painting
10 cm. Szentendre

GREY HORSE, 1940–45
Terracotta, turned, with engobe painting
23 cm. Szentendre

DISH WITH ANGEL, 1947
Terracotta, turned
30 cm. Owned by M. K.

"CHICKI", DISH, 1948
Terracotta, turned and painted
17 cm. Owned by M. K.

136

"FLUCTUAT NEC MERGITUR". JUG,
1948–49
Terracotta, turned, with engobe painting
and glazing
23 cm. Szentendre
(Ill. 134 and colour plates 21, 22)

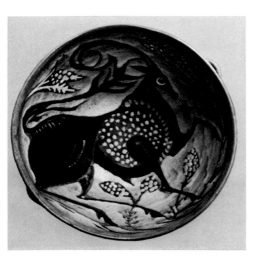

132

VASE WITH ARCHER, c. 1939
Terracotta, turned, engraved,
with engobe painting, signed "K. M."
66 cm. Szentendre

BEAKED PITCHER WITH BIRD-RELIEF,
1940
Terracotta, turned, with the inscription
"Anno Domini 1940"
44 cm. Owned by M. K.

LARGE VESSEL WITH TWO HANDLES,
c. 1940–42
Terracotta, turned, engraved
and ornamented with glazes
55 cm. Owned by M. K. (Ill. 130)

134

DISH WITH BULL, c. 1943–44
Terracotta, turned, with engobe painting
23 cm. Szentendre (Ill. 132)

DISH WITH HORSE, c. 1943–44
Terracotta, turned, with engobe painting
23 cm. Szentendre (Ill. 133)

FLAT FISH, c. 1945–50
Terracotta, turned, with engobe painting
29 cm. Szentendre

DISH WITH EVANGELIST, 1946–47
Terracotta, turned, with engobe painting
55 cm. Szentendre

137

DISH WITH LIZARD, 1949
Terracotta, turned, with glazing
58 cm. Szentendre
(Ill. 135 and colour plate 23)

STEMMED ROUND VASE, 1948
Terracotta, turned, painted
15 cm. Owned by M. K.

DISH WITH ANTELOPE, 1948
Turned, with engobe painting and glazing
30 cm. Owned by M. K.

STARTLED HEN, c. 1949
Terracotta, turned, with engobe painting
22 cm. Owned by M. K.

BULL, 1949–50
Terracotta, modelled, with engobe painting
and glazes, engraved ornamentation
44 cm. Szentendre

TORTOISE, 1949–50
Turned, with glazing
29 cm. Szentendre

DISH WITH VULTURE, 1950
Terracotta, turned, with glazes
55 cm. Szentendre
(Ill. 136 and colour plate 24)

LION, 1950
Terracotta, turned, with engobe painting
31 cm. Szentendre

POUTING FISH, 1950
Terracotta, turned, with engobe painting
16 cm. Szentendre

VASE WITH ROOSTER AND HEN I,
c. 1950
Terracotta, turned, with engobe painting
and glaze
32 cm. Owned by M. K.

138

VASE WITH ROOSTER AND HEN II,
c. 1950
Terracotta, turned, with engobe painting
and glaze
32 cm. Owned by M. K.

VASE WITH ROOSTER AND HEN III,
c. 1950
Terracotta, turned, with engobe painting
and glaze
32 cm. Owned by M. K.

ANGEL WITH OUTSTRETCHED WINGS,
c. 1950
Terracotta, turned, with engobe painting
58 cm. Szentendre

BIG WINE DISH, c. 1950
Turned, painted
29 cm. Owned by M. K.

DUCK, c. 1950
Terracotta, turned, with engraved
ornamentation
11 cm. Szentendre

139

PITCHER WITH WHITE AND BLUE
FLOWERS, c. 1950
Terracotta, turned, with glazing
26 cm. Szentendre
(Ill. 137 and colour plate 26)

140

SEATED RAM, c. 1950
Terracotta, turned, with glazing
18 cm. Szentendre

GUINEA-HEN, c. 1950
Terracotta, turned, modelled, with glazing
15 cm. Szentendre

BIRD WITH FISH, PLATTER, c. 1950
Terracotta, turned, with engobe painting,
signed "K. M."
30 cm. Szentendre (Ill. 138)

EMBRACING LIONS, c. 1950
Terracotta, turned, modelled
25 cm. Szentendre

141

DISH WITH VULTURE, c. 1950
Turned, painted
29 cm. Owned by M. K.

RED JUG WITH EAGLE, c. 1950
Terracotta, turned, signed "*K M 1950*"
26 cm. Owned by M. K.

VASE WITH GREEN FISH, 1950–51
Turned, painted
29 cm. Owned by M. K.

STAG WITH FLOWER, 1950–53
Terracotta, turned, with engobe painting
32 cm. Szentendre

142

DARK STAG, 1950–55
Terracotta, turned, with engobe painting
32 cm. Szentendre (Ill. 139)

PEACE JUG, 1951
Terracotta, turned, engobe painting,
glazed with inscription: "*KM 1951 Békekorsó*"
42 cm. Owned by M. K. (Ill. 140)

143

DISH WITH LID, 1951
Terracotta, turned, signed "*K M 1951*"
21 cm. Owned by M. K.

SEAL-COLOURED JUG, 1951
Terracotta, turned, signed "*Anno 1951 K M*"
22 cm. Owned by M. K.

GREEN DISH WITH BIRD'S HEAD, 1951
Terracotta, turned, engobe painted with glaze,
signed "*1951 K M*"
22 cm. Owned by M. K.

144

JONAH GOBLET, 1951
Terracotta, turned, with glazing, signed
"*Jónás-cápa K M*" (Jonah whale)
36 cm. Owned by M. K. (Ill. 141)

145

SMALL GREEN DISH WITH HANDLE, 1952
Terracotta, turned, with engobe painting,
and glazed. Signed "*1952 K M*"
14 cm. Owned by M. K.

PURPLE GOBLET WITH "K M", 1952
Terracotta, turned, signed "*K M*"
28 cm. Owned by M. K.

DISH WITH LION, 1952
Terracotta, turned with engobe painting
and glazed
31 cm. Owned by M. K.

146

TALE PITCHER, 1952
Terracotta, turned, engraved, engobe painting,
glazing, with inscription: "*Hol volt, hol nem
volt K M 1952*" (Once upon a time...)
81 cm. Szentendre (Ill. 142)

BIG PITCHER, 1952
Terracotta, turned, with engobe painting,
signed "*1952 K M*"
45 cm. Owned by M. K.

"MARCH JUG", 1952
Terracotta, turned, modelled, engraved with
glazing, signed "*Március K M*"
35 cm. Szentendre (Ill. 143)

BIG DISH WITH DUCK, c. 1952
Turned, painted
29 cm. Owned by M. K.

SPARROW JUG, c. 1952–53
Terracotta, turned, engraved, with engobe
painting
17 cm. Owned by M. K.

"THE PEACOCK ALIGHTED...", *DISH*,
1953
Terracotta, turned, modelled, engraved,
with engobe painting, glazed, with the
inscription "*1953 — Felszállott a páva
a vármegyeházra — Sok szegénylegénynek
szabadulására*" (The peacock alighted top
of County Hall—the outcasts and rebels
to free them all)
57 cm. Szentendre

147

PIGEON, 1953
Turned, painted
16 cm. Owned by M. K.

EAGLE WITH SERPENT, 1953
Terracotta, turned, with engobe painting,
glazed
31 cm. Owned by M. K.

BLACK EAGLE JUG, 1953
Terracotta, turned, with engraved
ornamentation
33 cm. Szentendre (Ill. 144)

FAT YELLOW JUG WITH FAT BIRD, c. 1953
Terracotta, turned
14 cm. Owned by M. K.

VASE WITH ROOSTER AND FLOWER,
1953–54
Terracotta, turned, signed "*K M*"
30 cm. Owned by M. K.

STRAIGHT VASE WITH PURPLE GRAPES,
1953–54
Terracotta, turned, with engobe painting
21 cm. Owned by M. K.

TERRACOTTA VASE WITH WHITE GLAZE,
c. 1953–54
Terracotta, turned, glazed
17 cm. Owned by M. K.

VASE, c. 1953–54
Terracotta, turned, glazed, signed *"K M"*
20 cm. Szentendre

VASE WITH ARCHER ON HORSEBACK,
1954
Turned, painted
70 cm. Owned by M. K.

JUG WITH ANIMAL HEAD, 1954
Terracotta, turned, with engobe painting,
signed *"K M"*
36 cm. Szentendre

RED-LINED JUG, 1954
Terracotta, turned, with engobe painting,
signed *"1954 K M"*
19 cm. Szentendre

RED JUG WITH STAGS OUTLINED
IN WHITE, c. 1954
Terracotta, turned
17 cm. Owned by M. K.

STEMMED VASE, 1954
Terracotta, turned, with engraved
ornamentation with the inscription
"Anno 1954"
26 cm. Owned by M. K.

PEACE DOVE, 1954
Terracotta, turned, with engobe painting
25 cm. Owned by M. K.

IVORY COLOURED VASE WITH FOWL,
1954–55
Terracotta, turned, signed *"K M"*
20 cm. Owned by M. K.

VASE WITH HEN, c. 1954–55
Turned, painted
32 cm. Owned by M. K.

COBALT-BLUE JUG, 1955
Terracotta, turned, with the inscription
"K M Anno 1955"
28 cm. Owned by M. K.

DISH WITH BLUE FISH, c. 1955
Terracotta, turned with engobe painting
31 cm. Owned by M. K.

SNARLING LION, 1957
Terracotta, turned, modelled, with
engobe painting and glazing, signed *"K M"*
37 cm. Szentendre (Ill. 145)

DRAGON, 1959
Terracotta, turned, modelled, with engobe
painting and glaze
32 cm. Szentendre

"SPRING WIND SWELLS THE WATER"—
DISH, c. 1960
Terracotta, turned, with engobe painting,
glazed
52 cm. Szentendre

BOY WITH STAG, c. 1960
Terracotta, with engraved ornamentation
35 cm. Owned by M. K.

"NOAH'S ARK" JUG, c. 1960
Terracotta, turned, with engraved
ornamentation, some glazing
40 cm. Owned by M. K. (Ill. 146)

SILENUS JUG, 1964
Terracotta, turned, modelled, with engobe
painting, inscription *"Silenus"*
25 cm. Szentendre

SYMBOL, 1965
Terracotta, turned, with engobe painting
48 cm. Szentendre

SHEPHERD'S JUG, 1967
Terracotta, turned, engobe painting, with
engraved ornamentation
62 cm. Szentendre

BAGPIPE PITCHER, 1968
Terracotta, turned, modelled, signed *"1968"*
50 cm. Szentendre (Ill. 147)

ANGELUS DISH, 1970
Terracotta, turned, with engobe painting
30 cm. Szentendre

FISHING ARCHANGEL, 1971
Chamotte clay, turned, with engobe painting,
engraved
50 cm. Szentendre

Printed in Hungary, 1979
Kossuth Printing House, Budapest
CO1765-h-7983
KA353-K-7983